Q: Skills for Success

5

LISTENING AND SPEAKING

Teacher's Handbook

Lawrence Lawson

OXFORD

UNIVERSITY PRESS

OXFORD
UNIVERSITY PRESS

198 Madison Avenue
New York, NY 10016 USA

Great Clarendon Street, Oxford, OX2 6DP, United Kingdom

Oxford University Press is a department of the University of Oxford.
It furthers the University's objective of excellence in research, scholarship,
and education by publishing worldwide. Oxford is a registered trade
mark of Oxford University Press in the UK and in certain other countries.

Photocopying

General Manager, American ELT: Laura Pearson
Publisher: Stephanie Karras
Associate Publishing Manager: Sharon Sargent
Associate Development Editors: Rebecca Mostov, Keyana Shaw
Director, ADP: Susan Sanguily
Executive Design Manager: Maj-Britt Hagsted
Associate Design Manager: Michael Steinhofer
Electronic Production Manager: Julie Armstrong
Production Artist: Elissa Santos
Cover Design: Michael Steinhofer
Production Coordinator: Elizabeth Matsumoto

ISBN: 978-0-19-475619-8 Listening and Speaking 5 Teacher's Handbook Pack
ISBN: 978-0-19-475662-4 Listening and Speaking 5 Teacher's Handbook
ISBN: 978-0-19-475667-9 Listening and Speaking 5/Reading and Writing 5
                        Testing Program CD-ROM
ISBN: 978-0-19-475643-3 Q Online Practice Teacher Access Code Card

Printed in China

This book is printed on paper from certified and well-managed sources.

ACKNOWLEDGMENTS
*The publishers would like to thank the following for their kind permission to reproduce
photographs:*
p. vi Marcin Krygier/iStockphoto; xiii Rüstem GÜRLER/iStockphoto

PREVIEW LISTENING 2

High-Tech Nomads

You are going to hear Rudy Maxa, host of the radio show *The Savvy Traveler*, interview reporter Joel Garreau about his research on a special group of businesspeople called *high-tech nomads*.

Check (✓) the descriptions you think would apply to a high-tech nomad.

☐ a self-employed businessperson

☐ a cyberspace traveler, rather than a plane traveler

☐ a worker who changes offices frequently

☐ a computer "geek"

☐ an employee who can't keep one job

☐ a worker who has an email address but no business address

 WHAT DO YOU THINK?

A. Discuss the questions in a group.

1. What do the speakers seem to think of the high-tech nomads? Do you agree with them? Why or why not?

2. Do you have the type of personality required to be a high-tech nomad? Do you have any interest in that sort of lifestyle? Why or why not?

3. In what ways do you try to be "wired" to the outside world? How much has your use of high-tech devices changed your daily life?

B. Think about both Listening 1 and Listening 2 as you discuss the question.

The reports described changes in the world around us (e.g., a lack of resources; an increase in technology). What other changes in today's world can you think of that could change the way some groups of people live, work, or study?

 One of the best features is your focus on developing materials of a high "interest level."
Troy Hammond, Tokyo Gakugei University, International Secondary School, Japan

Explicit skills instruction prepares students for academic success.

LANGUAGE SKILLS

Explicit instruction and practice in listening, speaking, grammar, pronunciation, and vocabulary skills **help students achieve language proficiency.**

LEARNING OUTCOMES

Practice activities allow students to **master the skills** before they are evaluated at the end of the unit.

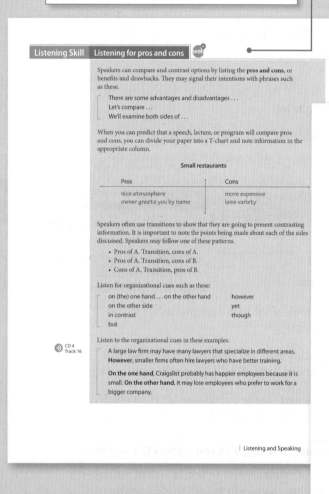

Listening Skill | **Listening for pros and cons**

Speakers can compare and contrast options by listing the **pros and cons**, or benefits and drawbacks. They may signal their intentions with phrases such as these.

There are some advantages and disadvantages . . .
Let's compare . . .
We'll examine both sides of . . .

When you can predict that a speech, lecture, or program will compare pros and cons, you can divide your paper into a T-chart and note information in the appropriate column.

Small restaurants

Pros	Cons
nice atmosphere	more expensive
owner greets you by name	less variety

Speakers often use transitions to show that they are going to present contrasting information. It is important to note the points being made about each of the sides discussed. Speakers may follow one of these patterns.

- Pros of A. Transition, cons of A.
- Pros of A. Transition, cons of B.
- Cons of A. Transition, pros of B.

Listen for organizational cues such as these:

on (the) one hand . . . on the other hand   however
on the other side   yet
in contrast   though
but

CD 4 Track 16

Listen to the organizational cues in these examples.

A large law firm may have many lawyers that specialize in different areas. **However**, smaller firms often hire lawyers who have better training.

On the one hand, Craigslist probably has happier employees because it is small. **On the other hand**, it may lose employees who prefer to work for a bigger company.

| Listening and Speaking

Speaking Skill | **Discussing preferences and alternatives**

In a meeting or a planning session, discussion often involves expressing preferences and offering alternatives. Additionally, you might need to investigate people's past preferences to help make choices about future actions.

Here are some common expressions for talking about preferences and alternatives.

To talk about past preferences	To talk about current preferences
prefer + noun or noun phrase Students **preferred** the expedition to China.	*preference* + *is* + infinitive **My preference is to attend** a science fair.
choose + infinitive Students **chose to visit** indigenous people.	*would rather (not)* + verb I'd **rather do** something that helps society.
first/second choice + *be* My **first choice was** to visit a nature reserve.	*If it were up to me, . . .* **If it were up to me,** we'd do an ecological study.
had hoped + infinitive I **had hoped to spend** the summer volunteering in Africa.	*I like . . . more than . . .* I like studying in my dorm **more than** in the lab.
	I'd like + verb **I'd like to explore** the idea of working abroad.

A. With a partner, take turns asking and answering these questions about the Listening texts. Use expressions for preferences and choices in your answers. Pay attention to your intonation in any choice questions.

1. Does Linda Stuart prefer the volunteering or the tourist side of voluntourism?

   A: *Does Linda Stuart prefer the volunteering or the tourist side of voluntourism?*
   B: *Stuart would rather be a volunteer than a tourist.*

2. Does Stuart's organization choose to take large or small groups of travelers?

3. If it were up to the speaker from Cambridge, would the science fair there have many more participants?

4. What does the professor at UC Santa Barbara hope to show the young students, especially girls?

 The tasks are simple, accessible, user-friendly, and very useful.
Jessica March, American University of Sharjah, U.A.E.

Q Online Practice provides all new content for additional practice in an easy-to-use online workbook. Every student book includes a *Q Online Practice access code card*. Use the access code to register for your *Q Online Practice* account at www.Qonlinepractice.com.

| Vocabulary Skill | Phrasal verbs | |

Phrasal verbs, made up of a verb followed by a **particle**, are a common type of collocation. The particle (usually a preposition or an adverb) following the verb changes the meaning. For example, *take on* does not have the same meaning as *take* or *take over*. Phrasal verbs are listed separately in learners' dictionaries and are marked with a symbol.

> **take sth/sb↔'on 1** to decide to do something; to agree to be responsible for something or someone: *I can't take on any extra work.* ♦ *We're not taking on any new clients at present.* **2** (of a bus, plane, or ship) to allow someone or something to enter: *The bus stopped to take on more passengers.* ♦ *The ship took on more fuel at Freetown.*

Some phrasal verbs take an object. A phrasal verb is **separable** if the object can be placed between the verb and the particle (*take* something *on*) as well as after it (*take on* something).

All dictionary entries are taken from the *Oxford Advanced American Dictionary for learners of English.*

A **research-based vocabulary program** focuses students on the words they need to know academically and professionally, using skill strategies based on the same research as the Oxford dictionaries.

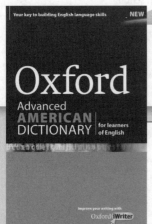

All dictionary entries are taken from the *Oxford Advanced American Dictionary for learners of English.*

The *Oxford Advanced American Dictionary for learners of English* was developed with English learners in mind, and provides extra learning tools for pronunciation, verb types, basic grammar structures, and more.

The Oxford 3000™ 🔑
The Oxford 3000 encompasses **the 3000 most important words to learn in English.** It is based on a comprehensive analysis of the Oxford English Corpus, a two-billion word collection of English text, and on extensive research with both language and pedagogical experts.

The Academic Word List AWL
The Academic Word List was created by Averil Coxhead and contains **570 words that are commonly used in academic English,** such as in textbooks or articles across a wide range of academic subject areas. These words are a great place to start if you are studying English for academic purposes.

QUICK GUIDE

Clear learning outcomes focus students on the goals of instruction.

LEARNING OUTCOMES

A culminating unit assignment evaluates the students' **mastery of the learning outcome.**

Unit Assignment | **Narrate a personal experience**

 In this section, you will narrate an experience involving language loss or an inability to communicate. As you prepare your narrative, think about the Unit Question, "How does language affect who we are?" and refer to the Self-Assessment checklist on page 50.

For alternative unit assignments, see the *Q: Skills for Success Teacher's Handbook.*

CONSIDER THE IDEAS

A. Maxine Hong Kingston, a Chinese-American writer, was born in the United States, but her parents spoke only Chinese at home. In her autobiographical novel, *The Woman Warrior*, she describes her discomfort speaking English after years of silence in American school and narrates a painful experience in Chinese school. Read this excerpt.

LEARNER CENTERED

Track Your Success allows students to **assess their own progress** and provides guidance on remediation.

Check (✓) the skills you learned. If you need more work on a skill, refer to the page(s) in parentheses.

LISTENING	I can listen for pros and cons. (p. 231)
VOCABULARY	I can use connotations. (p. 237)
GRAMMAR	I can use parallel structure. (p. 239)
PRONUNCIATION	I can speak with word stress patterns. (p. 241)
SPEAKING	I can develop interview skills. (p. 243)
LEARNING OUTCOME	I can role-play interviews for a job or a school and be prepared to answer a question that is creative or unusual.

 Students can check their learning ... and they can focus on the essential points when they study.

Suh Yoomi, Seoul, South Korea

For the student

- **Easy-to-use:** a simple interface allows students to focus on enhancing their speaking and listening skills, not learning a new software program
- **Flexible:** for use anywhere there's an Internet connection
- **Access code card:** a *Q Online Practice* access code is included with this book—use the access code to register for *Q Online Practice* at www.Qonlinepractice.com

For the teacher

- **Simple yet powerful:** automatically grades student exercises and tracks progress
- **Straightforward:** online management system to review, print, or export reports
- **Flexible:** for use in the classroom or easily assigned as homework
- **Access code card:** contact your sales rep for your *Q Online Practice* teacher's access code

Teacher Resources

Q Teacher's Handbook gives strategic support through:

- specific teaching notes for each activity
- ideas for ensuring student participation
- multilevel strategies and expansion activities
- the answer key
- special sections on 21st century skills and critical thinking
- a *Testing Program CD-ROM* with a customizable test for each unit

For additional resources visit the
Q: Skills for Success companion website at
www.oup.com/elt/teacher/Qskillsforsuccess

Q Class Audio includes:

- listening texts
- pronunciation presentations and exercises
- *The Q Classroom*

> It's an interesting, engaging series which provides plenty of materials that are easy to use in class, as well as instructionally promising.
> *Donald Weasenforth, Collin College, Texas*

UNIT	LISTENING	SPEAKING	VOCABULARY
1 New Media **Q How do people get the news today?** **LISTENING 1: Citizen Journalism** An Online Interview (Journalism) **LISTENING 2: Pod-Ready: Podcasting for the Developing World** A Podcast (Cultural Anthropology)	• Listen for the relationships between main ideas and details • Listen for specific vowel sounds • Predict content • Listen for main ideas • Listen for details	• Use note cards • Converse about advantages and disadvantages • Convey numerical information • Conduct a survey • Take notes to prepare for a presentation or group discussion	• Using the dictionary • Assess your prior knowledge of vocabulary
2 Language **Q How does language affect who we are?** **LISTENING 1: My Stroke of Insight: A Brain Scientist's Personal Journey** A Radio Interview (Neuroscience) **LISTENING 2: The Story of My Life** An Autobiography (Cognitive Science)	• Understand inferences • Listen for events in a chronology • Predict content • Listen for main ideas • Listen for details	• Use figurative language • Practice using word stress to emphasize ideas • Imply ideas instead of stating them directly • Narrate a story • Take notes to prepare for a presentation or group discussion	• Negative prefixes • Assess your prior knowledge of vocabulary
3 Work and Fun **Q Where can work, education, and fun overlap?** **LISTENING 1: Voluntourism** An Online Interview (Travel and Tourism) **LISTENING 2: Science Fairs and Nature Reserves** Academic Reports (Environmental Science)	• Listen for examples • Relate examples to main ideas • Formulate pre-listening questions about a topic • Predict content • Listen for main ideas • Listen for details	• Discuss preferences and alternatives • Use intonation to express choices and alternatives • Plan a persuasive presentation • Convince listeners to opt for one choice among many • Take notes to prepare for a presentation or group discussion	• Compound words • Assess your prior knowledge of vocabulary

GRAMMAR	PRONUNCIATION	CRITICAL THINKING	UNIT OUTCOME
• Participial adjectives	• Vowel variation with *a* and *o*	• Identify people/items that fit a definition • Interpret survey data • Assess your prior knowledge of content • Relate personal experiences to listening topics • Integrate information from multiple sources	• Develop and administer a survey focused on media preferences, analyze the results, and report your findings.
• Passive voice	• Emphatic word stress	• Contrast good and bad aspects of a situation • Experiment with brain stimuli • Assess your prior knowledge of content • Relate personal experiences to listening topics • Integrate information from multiple sources	• Develop a narrative incorporating figurative language that chronologically details an incident of language loss or an inability to communicate.
• Comparative structures	• Intonation with choices	• Identify personal preferences • Categorize activities • Assess your prior knowledge of content • Relate personal experiences to listening topics • Integrate information from multiple sources	• Plan and present a school vacation in a way that will persuade your classmates to select it for their spring break alternative trip.

UNIT	LISTENING	SPEAKING	VOCABULARY
4 Deception **Q** **How can the eyes deceive the mind?** **LISTENING 1:** Wild Survivors A Television Documentary (Zoology) **LISTENING 2:** Magic and the Mind A Radio Interview (Psychology)	• Recognize appositives that explain • Listen to identify word roots and suffixes • Predict content • Listen for main ideas • Listen for details	• Ask for and give clarification of information • Narrate incidents in your life • Explain reasons for opinions • Use relative clauses in a presentation • Take notes to prepare for a presentation or group discussion	• Word forms and suffixes • Assess your prior knowledge of vocabulary
5 Global Cooperation **Q** **What does it mean to be a global citizen?** **LISTENING 1:** The Campaign to Humanize the Coffee Trade A Radio Report (Business) **LISTENING 2:** The UN Global Compact A Report (Economics)	• Organize notes with a T-chart • Listen for problems and solutions • Listen for numbers • Predict content • Listen for main ideas • Listen for details	• Cite sources • Use numbers in presentations • Practice stress and intonation patterns in quoting directly from sources • Take notes to prepare for a presentation or group discussion	• Collocations • Assess your prior knowledge of vocabulary
6 Personal Space **Q** **How do you make a space your own?** **LISTENING 1:** Environmental Psychology A University Lecture (Psychology) **LISTENING 2:** What Your Stuff Says About You A Radio Interview (Social Psychology)	• Recognize organizational cues • Understand the overall structure of a passage • Predict content • Listen for main ideas • Listen for details	• Give advice • Practice conversational skills in an advice-giving situation • Take notes to prepare for a presentation or group discussion	• Words with multiple meanings • Assess your prior knowledge of vocabulary
7 Alternative Thinking **Q** **Where do new ideas come from?** **LISTENING 1:** Alternative Ideas in Medicine Radio Reports (Public Health) **LISTENING 2:** Boulder Bike-to-School Program Goes International A Radio Interview (Recreation and Fitness)	• Use a table to organize note-taking • Distinguish between facts and opinions • Predict content • Listen for main ideas • Listen for details	• Use formal and informal language • Practice persuading listeners to accept a new idea • Take notes to prepare for a presentation or group discussion	• Idioms and informal expressions • Assess your prior knowledge of vocabulary

GRAMMAR	PRONUNCIATION	CRITICAL THINKING	UNIT OUTCOME
• Relative clauses	• Stress shifts with suffixes	• Infer ideas from pictures • Speculate about a speaker's attitudes • Assess your prior knowledge of content • Relate personal experiences to listening topics • Integrate information from multiple sources	• Deliver a presentation that describes and gives examples of how optical illusions are used and discusses implications of their use.
• Reported speech	• Linking with final consonants	• Draw conclusions from pictures • Associate problems with solutions • Assess your prior knowledge of content • Relate personal experiences to listening topics • Integrate information from multiple sources	• Identify and report on aspects of a global problem.
• Conditionals	• Stress, intonation, and pauses to indicate thought groups	• Evaluate generalizations about groups of people • Draw conclusions from data • Assess your prior knowledge of content • Relate personal experiences to listening topics • Integrate information from multiple sources	• Role-play a talk show focused on identifying and solving conflicts centered on issues of personal space.
• Noun clauses	• Reduced sounds in conditional modals—affirmative and negative	• Identify personal thought processes • Evaluate the factual basis of ideas • Assess your prior knowledge of content • Relate personal experiences to listening topics • Integrate information from multiple sources	• Develop a marketing presentation designed to sell a new invention or idea.

UNIT	LISTENING	SPEAKING	VOCABULARY
8 Change **How do people react to change?** **LISTENING 1:** The Reindeer People A Radio Documentary (Cultural Anthropology) **LISTENING 2: High-Tech Nomads** A Radio Interview (Business)	• Recognize attitudes • Recognize meaning conveyed by intonation patterns • Predict content • Listen for main ideas • Listen for details	• Paraphrase • Speak about future plans and conditions • Conduct an interview • Take notes to prepare for a presentation or group discussion	• Phrasal verbs • Assess your prior knowledge of vocabulary
9 Energy **Where should the world's energy come from?** **LISTENING 1: Nuclear Energy: Is It the Solution?** A City Council Meeting (Public Policy) **LISTENING 2: Tapping the Energy of the Tides** A News Report (Engineering)	• Listen for cause and effect • Listen to associate ideas with different speakers • Predict content • Listen for main ideas • Listen for details	• Debate opinions • Converse informally about social issues • Take notes to prepare for a presentation or group discussion	• Greek and Latin word roots • Assess your prior knowledge of vocabulary
10 Size and Scale **Is bigger always better?** **LISTENING 1: Small Is the New Big** A Book Chapter (Business Management) **LISTENING 2: Sizing Up Colleges: One Size Does Not Fit All** A Podcast (Education)	• Listen for pros and cons • Listen for a speaker's attitudes • Listen for word stress and determine its impact on meaning • Predict content • Listen for main ideas • Listen for details	• Develop interview skills • Develop skills for answering interview questions • Take notes to prepare for a presentation or group discussion	• Connotations • Assess your prior knowledge of vocabulary

GRAMMAR	PRONUNCIATION	CRITICAL THINKING	UNIT OUTCOME
• Gerunds and infinitives	• Consonant variations	• Infer a speaker's attitudes • Hypothesize reasons why someone's attitudes changed • Assess your prior knowledge of content • Relate personal experiences to listening topics • Integrate information from multiple sources	• Interview a classmate and report on that person's attitudes concerning change.
• Adverb clauses	• Sentence rhythm	• Evaluate the feasibility of solutions to a problem • Assess your prior knowledge of content • Relate personal experiences to listening topics • Integrate information from multiple sources	• Participate in a class debate in which you support opinions concerning the future of energy.
• Parallel structure	• Word stress patterns	• Sort items into groups • Assess the usefulness of pieces of information • Assess your prior knowledge of content • Relate personal experiences to listening topics • Integrate information from multiple sources	• Role-play interviews for a job or a school and be prepared to answer a question that is creative or unusual.

Unit QUESTION
How do people get the news today?

New Media

LISTENING • identifying main ideas
VOCABULARY • using the dictionary
GRAMMAR • participial adjectives
PRONUNCIATION • vowel variation with *a* and *o*
SPEAKING • using note cards

LEARNING OUTCOME

Develop and administer a survey focused on media preferences, analyze the results, and report your findings.

▶ *Listening and Speaking 5, page 3*
Preview the Unit

Learning Outcome

1. Ask for a volunteer to read the unit skills, then the unit learning outcome.

2. Explain: *This is what you are expected to be able to do by the unit's end. The learning outcome explains how you are going to be evaluated. With this outcome in mind, you should focus on learning these skills (Listening, Vocabulary, Grammar, Pronunciation, Speaking) that will support your goal of "developing and administering a survey." This can also help you act as mentors in the classroom to help the other students meet this outcome.*

A (15 minutes)

1. Ask the class: *How many of you read or hear the news every day?* Of those who raised their hands, ask: *What kind of news stories do you follow? Why?* For those who didn't raise their hands, ask: *How do you find out what's going on in the world?*

2. Put students in pairs or small groups to discuss the first two questions.

3. Call on volunteers to share their ideas with the class. Ask questions: *Which media is the best to get the news—newspapers, the Internet, television, or radio? Why?*

4. Focus students' attention on the photo. Have a volunteer describe the photo to the class. Read the question aloud. Place students into pairs and have them discuss their answers to the questions. Have them give specific examples of the changes caused by new media.

Activity A Answers, p. 3
Possible answers:

1. When I want to know what is happening in the world, I search the Internet because websites have the most up-to-date information. I like to read newspapers because they have a lot of expert analysis that helps me understand current issues.

2. I evaluate if information is correct by asking my family and friends their opinions of the news I have read. Some news sources have better reputations for being fair and accurate in their reporting.

3. New technological devices, like iPads, allow us to get news faster than ever before.

B (10 minutes)

1. Introduce the Unit Question, "How do people get the news today?" Ask related information questions or questions about personal experience to help students prepare for answering the more abstract Unit Question. Ask students to brainstorm ways in which people got the news one hundred years ago (e.g., newspapers, radio, travelers, friends, etc.). Make a Venn diagram with the headings "News Sources in the Past" and "News Sources Today." Ask students to brainstorm current news sources (e.g., the Internet, television, newspapers, magazines, etc.) and list the sources in the appropriate sections of the diagram. Ask: *How are people in today's society consuming news differently than people consumed news one hundred years ago?*

2. Put students in small groups and give each group a piece of poster paper and a marker.

3. Read the Unit Question aloud. Give students a minute to silently consider their answers to the question. Tell students to pass the paper and the marker around the group. Direct each group member to write a different answer to the question. Encourage them to help one another.

4. Ask each group to choose a reporter to read the answers to the class. Point out similarities and differences among the answers. If answers from different groups are similar, make a group list that incorporates all of the answers. Post the list to refer to later in the unit.

Activity B Answers, p. 3
Possible answers: Today, people get the news instantly though text messages, email alerts, and the Internet. In modern times, not a lot of people pay attention to the news because they have many other distractions.

The Q Classroom (5 minutes)
CD1, Track 2

1. Play The Q Classroom. Use the example from the audio to help students continue the conversation. Ask: *How did the students answer the question? Do you agree or disagree with their ideas? Why?*

2. Say: *Felix notes that when there is important news, he watches the news on TV. Ask: Why do you think he says this? Is the news coverage on TV more important than the coverage in other sources?*

▶ *Listening and Speaking 5, page 4*

C (5 minutes)

1. Ask students to read over the survey.

2. Invite a volunteer to come to the front of the class to model how to complete the survey. Ask the volunteer the first two items on the survey, and record her answers on the board.

D (10 minutes)

1. Have students complete the surveys in groups.

2. When done, select students to share some of their answers to both the survey and their follow-up questions with the class.

MULTILEVEL OPTION

Pair lower- and higher-level students and have them create examples for each type of media listed in the survey. When it's time to share answers with the class, have them also share their examples.

EXPANSION ACTIVITY: Pros and Cons (15 minutes)

1. Say to students: *As we've been discussing, there are a variety of ways that people can get the news these days. Each method has distinct pros and cons. In this activity, I'd like to consider, list, and discuss the pros and cons of several news sources.*

2. Write the news sources discussed earlier on the board (e.g., *newspapers, magazines, the Internet, friends, travelers,* etc.)

3. Place students in groups of three and assign each group one or two news sources.

4. Direct each group to list the pros and cons of its assigned news source. Ask: *What makes it reliable? What are its limitations?*

5. After groups have finished conferring, as a class discuss and debate their results.

▶ *Listening and Speaking 5, page 5*

LISTENING

LISTENING 1: Citizen Journalism

Tip for Success (1 minute)

1. Ask a student to read the tip aloud.

2. Ask: *How can knowing the part of speech help you guess the meanings of words?*

VOCABULARY (15 minutes)

1. Model pronunciation of the bolded vocabulary words. Have students repeat each word three times.

2. Probe for prior knowledge by asking students if they have seen any of these vocabulary words before. If so, ask: *Where have you seen the word? What do you think it means?* Use student answers to preview answers in this vocabulary section.

3. Put students in groups of two or three, and have them complete the activity.

4. Ask different volunteers to read their vocabulary matches for the first four definitions. Have the class identify if the supplied vocabulary word was correct. If it wasn't, elicit a correction. Continue with the rest of the definitions.

MULTILEVEL OPTION

Pair lower- and higher-level students together, and have them create new sentences using several of the vocabulary words. Direct the higher-level students to make corrections to the sentences as needed. When students are finished, ask lower-level volunteers to write the sentences on the board for class consideration and discussion.

Vocabulary Answers, pp. 5–6

a. foundation b. viewpoint c. unique
d. networking e. accidental f. unfolding
g. accountable h. bias i. anonymous
j. technique k. upfront l. source

For additional practice with the vocabulary, have students visit *Q Online Practice*.

▶ *Listening and Speaking 5, page 6*

PREVIEW LISTENING 1 (5–10 minutes)

1. Direct students to look at the photo. Ask: *What is the person holding? How do you think this device relates to citizen journalism?*

2. Have a volunteer read the directions aloud, and direct students to complete the checklist individually.

3. Pair students and have them share their answers and elaborate on their experiences. Tell students they should review their answer after the Listening.

Listening 1 Background Note

There are several types of software that citizen journalists use to share information. A few free, popular blogging websites include Wordpress.com and Blogger.com. These services allow people to write and publish their views on the Internet. Often, people can publish right from their mobile telephones, so their followers can get up-to-the-minute news and reports.

Teaching Note

Students may find the following words or phrases difficult.

to the forefront (of something): (phr.) in or into an important or leading position in a particular group or activity

corporate: (adj.) connected with a corporations (a large business company)

transparency: (n.) the quality of something that allows somebody to see the truth easily, or the quality of a situation or argument that makes it easy to understand

expose: (v.) to show something that is usually hidden

cover: (n.) to report on an event for the news (also: *coverage*, noun)

explosion: (n.) a large, sudden, or rapid increase in the amount or number of something

LISTEN FOR MAIN IDEAS (10 minutes)

 CD1, Track 3

1. Preview the task by looking at item 1. Read the Host's question aloud, and direct students to read through the answers. Remind them that they'll select the answer that best represents the guest's answer in the audio.

2. Play the audio and have students complete the activity individually.

3. When done, review the questions with the class, having students raise left hands for "a" and right hands for "b." Ask the class to explain which answer was correct and why.

Listen for Main Ideas Answers, pp. 6–7
1. a **2.** b **3.** a **4.** a **5.** b

▶ *Listening and Speaking 5, page 7*

LISTEN FOR DETAILS (10 minutes)

 CD1, Track 4

1. Direct students to read the statements before they listen again.

2. As you play the audio, have students listen and select the best answer.

3. Have students compare answers with a partner.

4. Replay the audio so that partners can check their answers.

5. Go over the answers with the class.

Listen for Details Answers, pp. 7–8
1. c **2.** a **3.** c **4.** b **5.** a **6.** c

For additional practice with listening comprehension, have students visit *Q Online Practice*.

▶ *Listening and Speaking 5, page 8*

WHAT DO YOU THINK? (10 minutes)

1. Ask students to read the questions and reflect on their answers.

2. Seat students in small groups and assign roles: a group leader to make sure everyone contributes, a note-taker to record the group's ideas, a reporter to share the group's ideas with the class, and a timekeeper to watch the clock.

3. Give students five minutes to discuss the questions. Call time if conversations are winding down. Allow them an extra minute or two if necessary.

4. Call on each group's reporter to share ideas with the class.

What Do You Think? Answers, p. 8
Possible answers:

1. I think that citizen journalism can be more effective because there are no special interests dictating what that journalist reports. However, a citizen journalist might not have access to important sources of information that a traditional journalist does.

2. News organizations should employ more young people if they hope to produce content that will interest the young.

3. I think citizen journalism would be more popular in countries where the news media is run by the government because people would want to hear other points of view.

Learning Outcome

Use the learning outcome to frame the purpose and relevance of Listening 1. Ask: *What did you learn from Listening 1 that prepares you to develop and administer a survey?*

▶ *Listening and Speaking 5, page 9*

Listening Skill: Identifying main ideas
(20–25 minutes)

1. Present the information on the Listening Skill.

2. Check comprehension by asking questions: *What are some things to think about when looking for the main idea? (It's not always stated directly. It may follow the details. It may be stated first.) What types of phrases announce supporting details?*

3. Place students into groups. Have them brainstorm an outline of a news story where they include the **topic**, **main ideas**, and **details** of the story.

4. Discuss students' outlines as a class.

Tip for Success (1 minute)

Read the tip aloud. Review what **topic**, **main ideas**, and **details** are. Refer back to Listening 1 to elicit examples of each.

▶ *Listening and Speaking 5, page 10*

A (5–10 minutes)

1. Ask a student to read the directions aloud. Have students complete the activity with a partner.

2. Check answers as a class.

| **Listening Skill A Answers, p. 10**
| **1.** a **2.** b

B (5–10 minutes)

1. Ask a student to read the directions aloud. Have students complete the activity with a partner.

2. Check answers as a class.

| **Listening Skill B Answers, p. 10**
| **1.** D, 2 **2.** D, 4 **3.** D, 3 **4.** M, 1

C (5–10 minutes)
◉ CD1, Track 5

1. Ask a student to read the directions aloud.

2. Play the audio. Have students complete the activity individually.

3. Then play the audio again and have students check their answers.

4. Review answers as a class.

| **Listening Skill C Answers, pp. 10-11**
| **1.** a **2.** b **3.** d **4.** c

Critical Q: Expansion Activity

Apply (15 minutes)

1. Read the Critical Thinking Tip from page 10.

2. Write the following question on the board: How can you help your community learn important news and information? (e.g., I can access the Internet and tell the news I read to others who don't have Internet access or aren't members of online communities).

3. Place students into groups of three and have them apply the information they've learned in this unit so far in an answer to the above question. Encourage students to think of a realistic project that they could implement in their community.

 For additional practice with identifying main ideas, have students visit *Q Online Practice.*

LISTENING 2: Pod-Ready: Podcasting for the Developing World

VOCABULARY (20 minutes)

1. Before class, write several of the vocabulary words on slips of paper—one word per slip.

2. Ask students to study the spelling of the vocabulary words for three minutes. Then have students form groups of five and line up at the board in their groups, with one student in each group ready to write on the board.

3. Give the last person in each line a slip of paper. Instruct the student to tell the person in front of her the word to spell it. Then that student will pass the spelling on to the next person in the group, and so on. The person at the front of the line must write the word on the board.

4. Have students in each line rotate positions, and repeat the activity with as many words as desired.

5. When the activity is concluded, have students return to their seats and complete the vocabulary activity on pages 11–12 in pairs.

6. Check answers as a class.

> **Vocabulary Answers, pp. 11–12**
> **1.** b; **2.** c; **3.** c; **4.** b; **5.** a; **6.** a;
> **7.** c; **8.** c; **9.** b; **10.** b; **11.** a; **12.** a

 For additional practice with the vocabulary, have students visit *Q Online Practice*.

Tip for Success (1 minute)

Ask a student to read the tip aloud.

PREVIEW LISTENING 2 (5 minutes)

1. Direct students' attention to the photos and ask: *What do people use the device in the photo for? How can it be used to share news?*

2. Pair students and have them look through the checklist, selecting their answers.

3. Compare answers as a class. Call on volunteers to share ideas they added.

4. Tell students they should review their answers after the Listening.

Listening 2: Background Note

Practical Action is a charity based in the United Kingdom that seeks to reduce the effects of poverty on a community by giving more people access to technology—whether it is sophisticated technology like voice-recording software and computers or more basic forms such as simple electric generators. Practical Action was conceived by economist E.F. Schumacher in 1966. He saw that many areas in the world lacked resources to access and use technology.

Teaching Note

Students may find the following words or phrases difficult.

uptake: (n.) the process by which something is taken into a system; the rate at which this happens

agriculture: (n.) the science or practice of farming

initiative: (n.) a new plan for dealing with a particular problem or achieving a particular purpose

cultivation: (n.) the preparation and use of land for growing plants or crops

trundle: (v.) to move or roll somewhere slowly and noisily

LISTEN FOR MAIN IDEAS (15 minutes)

CD1, Track 6

1. Preview the questions with the class.

2. Pair students and have them predict what they think the answer to each question might be.

3. Play the audio and have students complete the activity individually.

4. Check answers as a class, and ask students to compare the correct answers with their predicted answers.

> **Listen for Main Ideas Answers, pp. 13–14**
> **1.** a **2.** c **3.** a **4.** b **5.** b

LISTEN FOR DETAILS (10 minutes)

CD1, Track 7

1. Direct students to read the statements before they listen again.

2. As you play the audio, have students listen and decide if the statements are true or false.

3. Have students compare answers with a partner and correct false statements.

4. Replay the audio so that partners can check their answers.

5. Go over the answers with the class.

> **Listen for Details Answers, pp. 14–15**
> 1. F; ICT stands for information and communication technology.
> 2. F; Podcasting started in about 2004.
> 3. T
> 4. T
> 5. F; Radio is a one-way medium.
> 6. F; You don't need a license to create a podcast.
> 7. F; Most people there make a living through agriculture.
> 8. T
> 9. T
> 10. T
> 11. F; The biggest barrier is the lack of electricity in remote areas.
> 12. T

 For additional practice with listening comprehension, have students visit *Q Online Practice*.

> **Listening and Speaking 5, page 15**

WHAT DO YOU THINK?

A (15 minutes)

1. Ask students to read the questions and reflect on their answers.

2. Seat students in small groups and assign roles: a group leader to make sure everyone contributes, a note-taker to record the group's ideas, a reporter to share the group's ideas with the class, and a timekeeper to watch the clock.

3. Give students five minutes to discuss the questions. Call time if conversations are winding down. Allow them an extra minute or two if necessary.

4. Call on each group's reporter to share ideas with the class.

> **Activity A Answers, p. 15**
> Possible answers:
> 1. These devices are cheap to own and, in many cases, families are used to using these technologies.
> 2. Yes, I think they could be part of the solution because some communities are successfully implementing them and, as the word spreads, perhaps more money will be invested.
> 3. The biggest obstacle is electricity and other sources of energy to power technology. The most exciting solution is to use audio players to educate young women as they work.

B (5 minutes)

1. Have students continue working in their small groups to discuss the questions in Activity B. Tell them to choose a new leader, recorder, reporter, and timekeeper.

2. Call on the new reporter to share the group's answers to the questions.

Learning Outcome

Use the learning outcome to frame the purpose and relevance of Listenings 1 and 2 and the Critical Q activity. Ask: *What did you learn from Listenings 1 and 2 and the Critical Q that prepares you to develop and administer a survey?*

> **Listening and Speaking 5, page 16**

Vocabulary Skill: Using the dictionary
(10 minutes)

1. Present the information on the Vocabulary Skill.

2. Check comprehension: *What kind of useful information can a learner's dictionary give you? What does* usage *refer to? What kinds of abbreviations might you find in the dictionary? What do they mean?*

Skill Note

Point out to students that while they may understand the meaning of new words, a lot more goes into actually using them in their own speech and writing. In addition to the meaning, pronunciation, and other information noted in the skill box, students need to know which words collocate, or are used with, words. Often, learners' dictionaries will include example collocations. Review this information with students and encourage them to practice trying out new vocabulary by using the words as part of collocations.

> **Listening and Speaking 5, page 17**

A (10 minutes)

1. Pair students and give each pair a dictionary.

2. Preview the directions to the activity, and ask students to complete the activity.

3. Go over the answers with the class.

> **Activity A Answers, p. 17**
> 1. inform
> 2. infinite
> 3. from
> 4. honest, frank
> 5. feasibility, noncount
> 6. key, vital

B (10 minutes)

1. Preview the directions with the class.
2. Model the activity by completing the first statement together.
3. Pair students and have them complete the activity.
4. Compare answers as a class and answer questions.

Activity B Answers, p. 17
1. to
2. the mainstream
3. to take
4. devices
5. idiom
6. countable

 For additional practice with using the dictionary, have students visit *Q Online Practice*.

▶ *Listening and Speaking 5, page 18*

SPEAKING

Grammar: Participial adjectives
(15 minutes)

1. Write a list of participial adjectives on the board (e.g., *breaking news, developed country, broken computer*) and a list of "regular" adjectives on the board (e.g., *intelligent girl, expensive car, blue sky*). Ask: *What makes these adjectives different from each other?* (Elicit that the first list looks similar to verbs while the second list does not.)

2. Present the information on the Grammar Skill. Point back to the original lists to highlight that participial adjectives come from the present or past participle of verbs.

3. Check comprehension by asking questions: *What ending does a present participle have? What kinds of endings do past participles have?*

Skill Note

Because a participial comes from the participle verb form, participial adjectives also feature regular and irregular forms. Therefore, present participial adjectives are not always formed with *–ing* (i.e. *forbidden news*), and past participial adjectives are not always formed with *–ed* (e.g., *mistaken identity*). When students are forming participial adjectives, remind them to be aware of regular and irregular verbs and to consult a dictionary if needed.

▶ *Listening and Speaking 5, page 19*

A (10 minutes)

1. Direct students to circle the correct adjective.
2. Put students in pairs to discuss their answers.
3. Call on volunteers to share their ideas aloud.

Activity A Answers, p. 19
1. interesting
2. written
3. approaching
4. downloaded
5. compelling
6. illustrated

B (20 minutes)

1. Have a volunteer read the directions to the activity.
2. As a class, brainstorm possible advantages and disadvantages.
3. Pair students and have them create their conversations.
4. Choose a few volunteers to share their conversations with the class.

 For additional practice with the participial adjectives, have students visit *Q Online Practice*.

▶ *Listening and Speaking 5, page 20*

Pronunciation: Vowel variation with *a* and *o* (15 minutes)

 CD1, Track 8

1. Probe students' prior knowledge by asking: *What do you find interesting (or frustrating) about the English vowel system?* (Lead them toward the idea that there are more sounds than letters.)

2. Check comprehension by asking questions: *What in your mouth can cause vowel sounds to change? What sounds can you make when your tongue is lowest in your mouth with your jaws and lips open wide? How many vowel sounds are in English?*

3. Play the audio and have students practice the different vowel sounds within the words.

▶ *Listening and Speaking 5, page 21*

A (15 minutes)

1. Preview the directions to the task.

2. Pair students and direct them to read the paragraphs aloud.

3. Have students read the paragraphs aloud again on their own, focusing on the vowel sounds in the bold words.

4. Choose a few students to read aloud.

B (15 minutes)

 CD1, Track 9

1. Preview the directions and direct students to complete the task individually.

2. Play the audio. Have students check their own pronunciation against the audio.

3. Have partners check answers. Then review the chart with the class.

> **Activity B Answers, p. 21**
> /eɪ/: agency, organizations, states, create, makes, radio, information; /æ/: aspects, happen, access, examples, accidental, practical, attractice; /ɑ/: blogging, common, documents, honest, watch, technology, podcasts, project, popular, on; /oʊ/: social, alone, moment, upload, also, don't, hopes, low, telephone, promote

C (10 minutes)

Pair students and direct them to ask and answer the questions together.

 For additional practice with vowel variation with *a* and *o*, have students visit *Q Online Practice*.

▶ *Listening and Speaking 5, page 22*

Speaking Skill: Using note cards
(10 minutes)

1. Probe for previous experience by asking: *Have any of you used note cards when giving a presentation? If so, were they helpful? Why or why not?*

2. Check comprehension: *What were some of the tips for preparing effective note cards? What were some of the tips for speaking with note cards?*

Tip for Success (2 minutes)

Read the tip aloud. Ask students to share any experience using PowerPoint.

▶ *Listening and Speaking 5, page 23*

A (15 minutes)

1. Preview the directions to the activity.

2. Pass out note cards.

3. Direct students to complete the task individually.

4. Pair students who chose the same topics. Ask them to compare their note cards and make any changes necessary.

B (15 minutes)

1. Pair students and direct them to complete the activity and then switch partners to present again. Circulate around the room, listening to, but not interrupting, the presentations.

2. Choose one or two students to present their topics to larger groups of students (or the whole class).

 For additional practice with using note cards, have students visit *Q Online Practice*.

Unit Assignment: Conduct a class survey

Unit Question (5 minutes)

Refer students back to the ideas they discussed at the beginning of the unit about how people get the news today. Cue students if necessary by asking specific questions about the content of the unit: *What are the advantages and disadvantages of different news sources? Where do you like to get your news? Why?*

Learning Outcome

1. Tie the Unit Assignment to the unit learning outcome. Say: *The outcome for this unit is to develop and administer a survey. In this Unit Assignment you will develop and administer a survey.*

2. Explain that you are going to use a rubric similar to their self-assessment rubric on p. 26 to grade their Unit Assignment. You can also share a copy of the Unit Assignment Rubric (on p. 12 of this *Teacher's Handbook*) with students.

Consider the Ideas (5–10 minutes)

1. Place students into groups of three, and have them consider the photo and answer the questions.

2. When done, briefly discuss answers as a class.

Prepare and Speak

Gather Ideas

A (25 minutes)

1. Have students work in their same groups of three to complete the activity.

2. Provide a few models of questions students might want to include in their surveys or ask as follow-up questions (e.g., *Do you get your news from the radio? Do you think news from the Internet is reliable?*). Direct students to begin writing their surveys.

3. Circulate around the room to provide support and model additional questions as needed.

4. Once their surveys are written, give students time to practice asking their questions. Then remind students that they should interview people outside of class.

▶ *Listening and Speaking 5, page 25*

Organize Ideas

B (25 minutes)

1. Preview the directions to the activity. Solicit questions students might have and review how to create note cards.

2. Place students into the same groups of three they've been working in to support each other as they complete the activity. Provide support as needed.

21ST CENTURY SKILLS

When students look at the results of their surveys and try to make sense of them for their presentations, they are using a valuable skill: the ability to analyze information. Encourage students to reflect on what the answers from the survey tell them about the people they interviewed. Write questions such as the following on the board: *What do the answers say about the people who you interviewed? Were you surprised by any answers? How do your own answers influence how you interpret these results?* Discuss answers as a class.

▶ *Listening and Speaking 5, page 26*

Speak

C (25–45 minutes)

1. Call on students to give their presentations to the class. Remind students to try to use at least five vocabulary words in their presentations.

2. Use the Unit Assignment Rubric on p. 12 of this *Teacher's Handbook* to score each student's presentation.

3. Alternatively, divide the class into large groups and have students give their presentations to their group. Have listeners complete the Unit Assignment Rubric.

Alternative Unit Assignments

Assign or have students choose one of these assignments to do instead of, or in addition to, the Unit Assignment.

1. Defend your choice for the best source for news in the 21st century: television reporters, newspaper reporters, citizen journalists, bloggers, or talk radio hosts.

2. Discuss the reasons some people might prefer not to tune in to radio and television talk shows for news and information.

3. Defend your agreement or disagreement with the motto of Korea's online newspaper *OhMyNews,* "Every citizen is a reporter."

4. Discuss the ways international organizations could improve the sharing of information and technology in developing countries.

 For an additional unit assignment, have students visit *Q Online Practice.*

Check and Reflect

Check

A (10 minutes)

1. Direct students to read and complete the self-assessment rubric.

2. Ask for a show of hands for how many students gave all or mostly *yes* answers.

3. Congratulate them on their success. Remind students that they can refer to the rubric before they begin the Unit Assignment so they can focus on the skills needed to do well. Have students discuss with a partner what they can improve.

B (5–10 minutes)

Ask students to consider the questions in pairs or groups of three. When the conversations have tapered off, ask: What was the most difficult part of this survey? Developing and giving it? Analyzing your results? Or reporting on your findings? Why?

▶ *Listening and Speaking 5, page 27*

Track Your Success (5 minutes)

1. Have students circle the words they have learned in this unit. Suggest that students go back through the unit to review any words they have forgotten.

2. Have students check the skills they have mastered. If students need more practice to feel confident about their proficiency in a skill, point out the page numbers and encourage them to review.

3. Read the Learning Outcome aloud. Ask students if they feel that they have met the outcome.

Unit Assignment Rubric

Student name: _____

Date: _____

20 points = Presentation element was completely successful (at least 90% of the time).
15 points = Presentation element was mostly successful (at least 70% of the time).
10 points = Presentation element was partially successful (at least 50% of the time).
 0 points = Presentation element was not successful.

Conduct a Class Survey	20 points	15 points	10 points	0 points
Student spoke clearly and used note cards appropriately.				
Student clearly articulated both main ideas and details.				
Student used participial adjectives correctly.				
Student used at least five vocabulary items from the unit.				
Student pronounced vowels correctly.				

Total points: _____

Comments:

Unit QUESTION

How does language affect who we are?

Language

LISTENING • making inferences
VOCABULARY • negative prefixes
GRAMMAR • passive voice
PRONUNCIATION • emphatic word stress
SPEAKING • using figurative language

LEARNING OUTCOME

Develop a narrative incorporating figurative language that chronologically details an incident of language loss or an inability to communicate.

▶ *Listening and Speaking 5, page 29*

Preview the Unit

Learning Outcome

1. Ask for a volunteer to read the unit skills, then the unit learning outcome.

2. Explain: *This is what you are expected to be able to do by the unit's end. The learning outcome explains how you are going to be evaluated. With this outcome in mind, you should focus on learning these skills (Listening, Vocabulary, Grammar, Pronunciation, Speaking) that will support your goal of "developing a narrative about language loss." This can also help you act as mentors in the classroom to help the other students meet this outcome.*

A (10 minutes)

1. Ask: *In your home country, can a tourist do everything using only English? (e.g., buy train tickets)*

2. Put students in pairs or small groups to discuss the first two questions.

3. Call on volunteers to share their ideas with the class. Ask questions: *Are there some expressions in your native language that can't be translated into other languages? Have you had any experiences with tourists in this country?*

4. Focus students' attention on the photo. Have a volunteer describe the photo to the class. Read the question aloud. Place students into pairs and have them discuss the questions. Call on volunteers to share their answers.

Activity A Answers, p. 29
Possible answers:
1. An English speaker would have a hard time finding someone who understood English.
2. I think that people have different thoughts because the way you construct thoughts in different languages is different and may make the actual thoughts different.

3. They are communicating by talking, but what they are saying is being interpreted by someone else and played through the earphones in the photo. Another non-standard communication is sign language.

B (10 minutes)

1. Introduce the Unit Question, "How does language affect who we are?" Ask related questions to help students prepare for answering the more abstract Unit Question: *Does the language you speak affect your personality? Do you act differently when you use a different language? If so, what differences do you see?*

2. Read the Unit Question aloud. Point out that answers to the question can fall into categories (personality, perception, communication patterns, and relationships). Give students a minute to silently consider their answers to the question.

3. Write each category at the top of a sheet of poster paper. Elicit answers for the question and make notes of the answers under the correct heading. Post the lists to refer to later in the unit.

Activity B Answers, p. 29
Possible answers: The language we use shows people who we are. Language allows us to express our personalities. We use language to identify with certain groups. The languages we speak influence how we interpret the world.

The Q Classroom (5 minutes)

🔊 CD1, Track 10

1. Play The Q Classroom. Use the example from the audio to help students continue the conversation. Ask: *How did the students answer the question? Do you agree or disagree with their ideas? Why?*

2. Say: *In the audio, Marcus says that language is a part of culture. Do you agree? Why or why not?*

Activity A Answers, p. 40
Possible answers:

1. I think a child like Helen Keller should learn in a school setting so she could learn how to be around other people. I think such a child would be more successful with a private tutor because a tutor could attend to that child's needs.
2. I think it is hard to put love into words; everything you can say doesn't seem good enough. I think people express love with actions instead of words.
3. Before her teacher came, she was a frustrated person because she was unable to communicate her thoughts. However, after her teacher came, she was much happier because she was given the gift of language.

B (5 minutes)

1. Have students continue working in their small groups to discuss the questions in Activity B. Tell them to choose a new leader, recorder, reporter, and timekeeper.
2. Call on the new reporter to share the group's answers to the questions.

Learning Outcome

Use the learning outcome to frame the purpose and relevance of Listenings 1 and 2 and the Critical Q activity. Ask: *What did you learn from Listenings 1 and 2 and the Critical Q that prepares you to develop a narrative about language loss?*

▶ *Listening and Speaking 5, page 41*

Vocabulary Skill: Negative prefixes
(5–10 minutes)

1. Probe for previous knowledge by asking: *What is a prefix? What are some examples of prefixes?*
2. Present the information on the Vocabulary Skill.
3. Check comprehension: *What are examples of negative prefixes? What's a pattern for* il-? *What's a pattern for* ir-?

Tip for Success (1 minute)

Ask a volunteer to read the tip aloud. Have students repeat the words *unimportant* and *dysfunctional* aloud.

Skill Note

Learning prefixes is an excellent way for students to expand, or even double, their vocabulary without learning completely new words. Emphasize to students that by adding the correct prefix to adjectives they already know, or are learning, they can learn two or more words with one effort.

EXPANSION ACTIVITY: Negative Prefixes (15 minutes)

1. To provide practice with negative prefixes, place students in groups of four, and provide them with a stack of ten cards, each with a different adjective written on it (e.g., *legal, capable, regular, satisfied, decided, ending, logical, relevant,* and *reliable*).
2. Write the negative prefixes on the board.
3. Have students match the adjective to the correct prefix and create a sentence with the new word, taking turns sharing their sentences aloud.
4. Practice stressing the negative meaning the prefixes carry by having a student create a sentence with the original adjective, and then having the next student say a sentence with the adjective plus the prefix.

A (10 minutes)

1. Preview the instructions and model the activity by completing the first item together.
2. Place students into pairs to complete the activity.
3. Go over the answers with the class.

Activity A Answers, pp. 41–42
1. disconnected   2. unconscious
3. irregular   4. unaware
5. insensitive   6. impatient

▶ *Listening and Speaking 5, page 42*

B (10 minutes)

1. As a class, brainstorm descriptions of the two women. Ask: *How would you describe Helen Keller? Jill Bolte Taylor?*
2. Preview the instructions. Have students complete the activity and then compare sentences in pairs.

MULTILEVEL OPTION

Pair higher- and lower-level students and have the higher-level students review the meanings of the adjectives after the prefix has been added.

 For additional practice with negative prefixes, have students visit *Q Online Practice*.

▶ *Listening and Speaking 5, page 43*

SPEAKING

Tip for Success (3 minutes)

1. Ask a volunteer to read the tip aloud.
2. Invite volunteers to provide another example sentence that is not passive but uses *be*.

Consider the Ideas

A (5 minutes)

Preview the instructions and direct students to read the passage individually. Ask students to underline vocabulary words they are unfamiliar with for discussion after the reading.

▶ *Listening and Speaking 5, page 49*

B (10 minutes)

Place students in groups of four, and have them discuss the questions and their answers. Continue the discussion as a class. Review meanings of any unfamiliar words students identified above.

Prepare and Speak

Gather Ideas

A (10–15 minutes)

1. Have students work in their same groups of four to complete the activity. Review briefly a few stories from the unit to use as inspiration.

2. Circulate around the room to provide support and extended modeling as needed.

▶ *Listening and Speaking 5, page 50*

Organize Ideas

B (15–20 minutes)

1. Preview the instructions, and split groups up into pairs. Have each student create a story time line.

2. As students practice telling their narratives to each other, circulate around the room to ensure students are using the skills listed. Model as needed.

Speak

C (15–25 minutes)

1. Call on students to tell their narratives to the class.

2. Use the Unit Assignment Rubric on p. 22 of this *Teacher's Handbook* to score each student's presentation.

3. Alternatively, divide the class into large groups and have students tell their stories to their group. Have listeners complete the Unit Assignment Rubric.

Alternative Unit Assignments

Assign or have students choose one of these assignments to do instead of, or in addition to, the Unit Assignment.

1. Analyze some of the coping strategies people use when they are unable to communicate effectively.

2. Discuss your perception of the progress society has made in accepting people who are language-disabled. What more can we do?

3. Describe any differences in the way you communicate in your first and second languages.

 For an additional unit assignment, have students visit *Q Online Practice.*

Check and Reflect

Check

A (10 minutes)

1. Direct students to read and complete the self-assessment rubric.

2. Ask for a show of hands for how many students gave all or mostly *yes* answers.

3. Congratulate them on their success. Remind students that they can refer to the rubric before they begin the unit assignment so they can focus on the skills needed to do well. Have students discuss with a partner what they can improve.

Reflect

B (10 minutes)

Ask students to consider the questions in pairs or groups of three. When the conversations have tapered off, ask: *What did you enjoy most about developing this narrative? Why? What did you enjoy the least? Why?*

▶ *Listening and Speaking 5, page 51*

Track Your Success (5 minutes)

1. Have students circle the words they have learned in this unit. Suggest that students go back through the unit to review any words they have forgotten.

2. Have students check the skills they have mastered. If students need more practice to feel confident about their proficiency in a skill, point out the page numbers and encourage them to review.

3. Read the Learning Outcome aloud. Ask students if they feel that they have met the outcome.

Unit Assignment Rubric

Student name: _____

Date: _____

20 points = Presentation element was completely successful (at least 90% of the time).
15 points = Presentation element was mostly successful (at least 70% of the time).
10 points = Presentation element was partially successful (at least 50% of the time).
 0 points = Presentation element was not successful.

Narrate a Personal Experience	20 points	15 points	10 points	0 points
Student spoke clearly and at a good speed about the topic.				
Student used negative prefixes correctly.				
Student used active and passive voice appropriately.				
Student used several similes and metaphors.				
Student used appropriate word emphasis.				

Total points: _____

Comments:

UNIT

3

Unit QUESTION
Where can work, education, and fun overlap?

Work and Fun

LISTENING • listening for examples
VOCABULARY • compound words
GRAMMAR • comparative structures
PRONUNCIATION • intonation with choices
SPEAKING • discussing preferences and alternatives

LEARNING OUTCOME

Plan and present a school vacation in a way that will persuade your classmates to select it for their spring break alternative trip.

▶ *Listening and Speaking 5, page 53*
Preview the Unit

Learning Outcome

1. Ask for a volunteer to read the unit skills, then the unit learning outcome.

2. Explain: *This is what you are expected to be able to do by the unit's end. The learning outcome explains how you are going to be evaluated. With this outcome in mind, you should focus on learning these skills (Listening, Vocabulary, Grammar, Pronunciation, Speaking) that will support your goal of "presenting a school vacation plan." This can also help you act as mentors in the classroom to help the other students meet this outcome.*

A (10 minutes)

1. Ask the class: *When's the last time that you took a vacation? Should people get more vacation time from work? Why or why not?*

2. Put students in pairs or small groups to discuss the first two questions.

3. Call on volunteers to share their ideas with the class. Ask questions: *What can make work or school fun? When do you know that it's time to take a vacation?*

4. Focus students' attention on the photo. Have a volunteer describe the photo to the class. Read the question aloud. Have students look at the photo and answer the question in small groups. Discuss answers as a class. Have students list the details in the photo that helped them determine their answer.

Activity A Answers, p. 53
Possible answers:
1. The first factor I consider is what type of vacation I want—if I want to relax or explore a new place.
2. Work is fun when we work in teams to complete a project. School is fun when our teachers make us laugh.
3. The man is camping and having fun/Based on the equipment he has, I think he is doing work.

B (10 minutes)

1. Introduce the Unit Question, "Where can work, education, and fun overlap?" Ask related questions to help students prepare for answering the more abstract Unit Question: *Is it a good thing to have fun at school or work? Why or why not? What do you do to have a little bit of fun at school or work?*

2. Read the Unit Question aloud. Tell students: *Let's start off our discussion by listing ways in which work, education, and school can overlap.*

3. Seat students in small groups and direct them to pass around a paper as quickly as they can, with each group member adding one item to the list. Tell them they have two minutes to make the lists and they should write as many words as possible.

4. Call time and ask a reporter from each group to read the list aloud.

5. Use items from the list as a springboard for discussion. Say: *Let's talk about how having more breaks at work can be fun and productive.*

Activity B Answers, p. 53
Possible answers:
These areas can overlap when people laugh. Education, work, and fun can come together when people enjoy what they do.

The Q Classroom (5 minutes)

CD1, Track 18

1. Play The Q Classroom. Use the example from the audio to help students continue the conversation. Ask: *How did the students answer the question? Do you agree or disagree with their ideas? Why?*

2. Say: *In the audio, Felix says that "fun can be educational." What support does he give for this idea? Do you agree with him? Can fun be educational?*

▶ *Listening and Speaking 5, page 54*

Critical Q: Expansion Activity

Diagram (10 Minutes)

1. Read the Critical Thinking Tip from page 54.
2. Ask the class: *Have you made Venn diagrams before?* If so, ask: *When? Did you find them useful? Why?* If no one has made a Venn diagram before, briefly explain the process and show an example on the board.
3. Place students into pairs and ask them to label a T-chart with the headings *Volunteer Work* and *Vacation.* Then have students brainstorm places that fit into these categories and write them in the appropriate sides of the T-chart. Have students share answers as a class.
4. After students share their lists, point out that places that appear on both lists are items that would go in the middle of a Venn diagram. Tell students that they can use these lists later in the unit to work on their Unit Assignment.

C (10 minutes)

1. Preview the instructions and model how to complete the activity by placing the first item, "appreciate cultures," into the Venn diagram.
2. Direct students to place the phrases into the Venn diagram individually.

MULTILEVEL OPTION

Pair lower- and higher-level students to work together to place the items into the Venn diagram. Have them note any differences in opinions.

D (5–10 minutes)

Place students in groups of four to compare answers, and then discuss answers as a class.

▶ *Listening and Speaking 5, page 55*

LISTENING

LISTENING 1: Voluntourism

VOCABULARY (10 minutes)

1. Choose a volunteer to read each statement. Then as a class, match each vocabulary item with its corresponding definition.
2. Call on volunteers to tell how they determined the answers.

MULTILEVEL OPTION

Pair lower- and higher-level students together to read through the statements and match the vocabulary items with the definitions. Check answers as a class.

Vocabulary Answers, pp. 55–56
a. preservation
b. validate
c. immerse myself in
d. diverse
e. expedition
f. prompt
g. demographics
h. enticing
i. range
j. indigenous
k. raise awareness of
l. ecological

 For additional practice with the vocabulary, have students visit *Q Online Practice.*

▶ *Listening and Speaking 5, page 56*

PREVIEW LISTENING 1 (5 minutes)

1. Direct students to look at the photo. Ask: *Does what the people are doing in the photo match your idea of what a vacation is? Why or why not?*
2. Discuss the meaning of *amateur.* Direct students to read and answer the question. Tell students they should review their answer after the Listening.

Listening 1 Background Note

The Global Citizens Network is an organization that organizes trips for people who are interested in doing some good while they are vacationing. The organization, founded in 1992, organizes projects, such as building community parks and offering health care presentations. They believe that they add to the voluntourism experience by encouraging their participants to build lasting, sustainable relationships with the local people they work with.

Teaching Note

Students may find the following words or phrases difficult.

solicit: (v.) to try to persuade somebody to do something

baby boomers: (n.) the generation born after the Second World War; many more babies than usual are born during a baby boom.

versus: (prep.) a word used to compare two different ideas, choices, people, etc.

mass: (n.) a large amount or quantity; before a noun (mass tourism), affecting or including a large number of people or things

resonate: (v.) to remind somebody of something; to be similar to what somebody thinks or believes

LISTEN FOR MAIN IDEAS (10 minutes)

 CD1, Track 19

1. Preview the instructions and the questions together as a class.
2. Play the audio and have students complete the activity individually.
3. Place students into pairs and have them check their answers.

> **Listen for Main Ideas Answers, pp. 56–57**
> Answers will vary but may include:
> 1. To provide an opportunity for people to travel and do service work by offering cross-cultural trips.
> 2. Stuart would say that women make up most of the volunteers, that the average age is 30 to 55, and that many people go to meet people and learn a new language.
> 3. Travelers get to contribute to society while experiencing new cultures. Countries get aid in completing projects, education, and special programs.

Tip for Success (3 minutes)

Have a volunteer to read the tip aloud. Ask: *What other abbreviations and acronyms do you know?*

▶ *Listening and Speaking 5, page 57*

LISTEN FOR DETAILS (10 minutes)

 CD1, Track 20

1. Direct students to fill out the Web page with information they remember from Listening 1 before they listen again.
2. As you play the audio, have students listen and fill in items they missed.
3. Have students compare answers with a partner.
4. Replay the audio so that partners can check their answers.
5. Go over the answers with the class.

> **Listen for Details Answers, p. 57**
> 1. Serving the volunteer tourist for over <u>16</u> years
> 2–3. Average age range <u>30</u> to <u>55</u>
> 4–5. Trip length <u>1</u> to <u>3</u> weeks
> 6–7. Average group size <u>4</u> to <u>12</u> people
> 8–9. Fees range $<u>900</u> to $<u>2,400</u>
> 10. working on <u>construction</u> of a health center
> 11. teaching <u>English</u>
> 12. helping indigenous groups preserve their <u>culture</u>
> 13–14. practice <u>a new language</u>, try <u>new foods</u>
> 15–17. We have programs around the world in urban and <u>rural</u> areas, in Mexico, Ecuador, <u>Peru</u>, <u>Guatemala</u>, <u>Africa</u> and <u>Asia</u>, <u>Kenya</u> and <u>Tanzania</u>, <u>Nepal</u> and <u>Thailand</u> (any of the listed places are correct).

 For additional practice with listening comprehension, have students visit *Q Online Practice*.

21ST CENTURY SKILLS

Working with others involves communicating new ideas. Use the concept of voluntourism to practice this skill. Ask students to explain the concept of voluntourism to friends, relatives, community members, or other students. Then have students ask the listener how voluntourism might benefit their community. Invite students to share their results with the class. The quality of students' answers may help you assess whether or not they communicated the idea of voluntourism effectively.

WHAT DO YOU THINK? (10 minutes)

1. Ask students to read the questions and reflect on their answers.

2. Seat students in small groups and assign roles: a group leader to make sure everyone contributes, a note-taker to record the group's ideas, a reporter to share the group's ideas with the class, and a timekeeper to watch the clock.

3. Give students five minutes to discuss the questions. Call time if conversations are winding down. Allow them an extra minute or two if necessary.

4. Call on each group's reporter to share ideas with the class.

MULTILEVEL OPTION

Place students in groups of four, with two higher-level students and two lower-level students. Have one higher-level student interview the two lower-level students using the questions from "What Do You Think?" and have the other higher-level student record their answers to share with the class.

What Do You Think? Answers, p. 58
Possible answers:
1. What she means by "it's us all together" is that everyone needs to take care of our world. I agree. I think that just as important as the project are the relationships formed.
2. I'll definitely consider it when I'm older. I think it'd be fun to do with friends from college.
3. I think my country can benefit from voluntourism; volunteers could teach technology classes.

Learning Outcome

Use the learning outcome to frame the purpose and relevance of Listening 1. Ask: *What did you learn from Listening 1 that prepares you to present a school vacation plan?*

Listening Skill: Listening for examples
(10 minutes)

 CD1, Track 21

1. Present the information in the Listening Skill box. Play the highlighted audio at the appropriate time.

2. Check comprehension. Ask: *What strategies can you use to listen for examples? What note-taking strategy is discussed here?*

A (10 minutes)

 CD1, Track 22

1. Ask a volunteer to read the instructions and the main points aloud.

2. Play the audio and direct students to fill in the examples as they listen.

3. Pair students to compare answers; then check answers as a class.

Listening Skill A Answers, p. 59
1. physical labor, health clinics, schools, community centers
2. giving back, contributing, sharing meaningful experience with family
3. United States, Canada, Mexico, Ecuador, Peru, Guatemala, Kenya, Tanzania, Nepal, and Thailand

B (10 minutes)

Pair students and direct them to interview each other using the questions.

For additional practice with listening for examples, have students visit *Q Online Practice*.

LISTENING 2: Science Fairs and Nature Reserves

VOCABULARY (20 minutes)

1. Read the directions. Demonstrate how to complete the activity by reading the first sentence along with the definitions for the bolded word. Discuss the answer choices and, as a class, review the answer.

2. Put students into groups of three and assign roles: one reader, one decider, and one writer. The reader reads the sentence, the group discusses the correct answer, the decider makes the final decision, and the writer writes the answer.

3. Check answers as a class.

Vocabulary Answers, pp. 59–61
1. a 2. a 3. b 4. b 5. a 6. a
7. b 8. a 9. b 10. a 11. b 12. a

For additional practice with the vocabulary, have students visit Q Online Practice.

▶ *Listening and Speaking 5, page 61*

PREVIEW LISTENING 2 (5 minutes)

1. Direct students' attention to the photos and ask: *How does this photo help you understand what a nature reserve is?*

2. Discuss what a science fair and nature reserve are. Direct students to write information questions as instructed. Tell students they should review their questions after the Listening.

Listening 2 Background Note

The Sedgwick Nature Reserve is located on the central coast of California and is host to many research, artistic, and educational activities. The land was designated a nature preserve in 1996, after many years of life as a private ranch, and is a popular field trip destination for local schools, as one of the reports in Listening 2 will show. The natural ecosystem consists of microscopic organisms, plants, animals, weather patterns, and land that coexist and provide a sustainable habitat for members of that ecosystem.

Teaching Note

Students may find the following words or phrases difficult.

staid: (adj.) not amusing or interesting; boring or old-fashioned

squelch: (v.) to make a wet, sucking sound

innovative: (adj.) introducing or using new ideas or ways of doing something

microorganism: (n.) a very small living thing that you can only see under a microscope

docent: (n.) a person whose job it is to show tourists around a museum or other place, and to talk about it

county: (n.) an area of the U.S. that has its own government

anatomy: (n.) the scientific study of the structure of human or animal bodies or plants

generate: (v.) to produce or create something

botany: (n.) the scientific study of plants and their structure

K through 12: (phr.) Kindergarten through Grade 12 (the last year in an American secondary school) – the school grades covering approximate ages five through eighteen

LISTEN FOR MAIN IDEAS (20 minutes)

 CD1, Track 23

A (10 minutes)

1. Preview the instructions and ask: *What will you be taking notes about?*

2. Play the audio and have students complete the activity individually.

3. Pair students to have them compare answers. Then discuss answers as a class.

> **Listen for Main Ideas A Answers, pp. 61–62**
> Answers may vary.

▶ *Listening and Speaking 5, page 62*

B (10 minutes)

1. Preview the instructions and model the activity by having the class construct an answer to the first question together.

2. Direct students to complete the rest of the activity individually.

3. Place students into groups of four to discuss their answers.

> **Listen for Main Ideas B Answers, p. 62**
> **1.** (1) To relate science to the real world, (2) to make more students interested in becoming scientists
> **2.** Any of these: the hands-on experiments are fun but also serious; they cause children to think about science in everyday life; they break down the barriers between scientists, research, and the community; students get to experience the science and realize they can become scientists
> **3.** Public outreach is bridging the gap between the university and the public. In both cases, professors want to involve the community in their work so people can appreciate it and so young people can pursue it.

▶ *Listening and Speaking 5, page 63*

LISTEN FOR DETAILS (10 minutes)

 CD1, Track 24

1. Direct students to preview the details before they listen again.

2. As you play the audio, have students listen and place the details into the Venn diagram.

3. Have students compare answers with a partner.

4. Replay the audio so that partners can check their answers.

5. Go over the answers with the class.

Listen for Details Answers, p. 63
Cambridge: b. in school buildings; d. geology and engineering; h. week-long event; i. over 45,000 visitors;
Segwick Reserve: a. botany and biology; k. year-long experience
Both: c. students from all grades; e. inspires interest in science; f. interactive activities; g. open to the public; j. praised by teachers

 For additional practice with listening comprehension, have students visit *Q Online Practice.*

WHAT DO YOU THINK?

A (10 minutes)

1. Ask students to read the questions and reflect on their answers.

2. Seat students in small groups and assign roles: a group leader to make sure everyone contributes, a note-taker to record the group's ideas, a reporter to share the group's ideas with the class, and a timekeeper to watch the clock.

3. Give students five minutes to discuss the questions. Call time if conversations are winding down. Allow them an extra minute or two if necessary.

4. Call on each group's reporter to share ideas with the class.

Activity A Answers, p. 63
Possible answers:
1. I'd be more interested in participating in programs at Sedgwick because I enjoy being outside.
2. Teachers should be concerned that students are learning as much as they can because there is a limited amount of school hours per day, and students need to master content.

B (5 minutes)

1. Have students continue working in their small groups to discuss the questions in Activity B. Tell them to choose a new leader, recorder, reporter, and timekeeper.

2. Call on the new reporter to share the group's answers to the questions.

Learning Outcome

Use the learning outcome to frame the purpose and relevance of Listenings 1 and 2. Ask: *What did you learn from Listenings 1 and 2 that prepares you to present a school vacation plan?*

▶ *Listening and Speaking 5, page 64*

Vocabulary Skill: Compound words
(10 minutes)

1. Present the information on the Vocabulary Skill.

2. Check comprehension: *What are common forms of compounds? What's an example of a compound noun? A compound adjective?*

Skill Note

It can be difficult for students to distinguish the parts of speech of compound nouns. Sometimes a word functions as a different part of speech when it is part of a compound. For example, *fiction* (an adjective) can be a noun in the compound noun *fiction writer*—even though *fiction* still seems to act as an adjective.

EXPANSION ACTIVITY: Compound Words
(15 minutes)

1. The English language is expanding as English users combine words to create new ones. Have students try this out by creating new compound words.

2. Place students into pairs and provide them with a list of 15 nouns and 15 adjectives of your choice.

3. Direct students to create new compound words (adjective/noun or noun/noun pairs) using their lists and to craft definitions for their new words.

4. Ask students to share some of their new words and definitions with the class. Choose a few words to use during the semester as "class words."

▶ *Listening and Speaking 5, page 65*

A (5–10 minutes)

1. Pair students and have them match the words to form compound words, then name the part of speech of their newly formed words.

2. Go over the answers with the class.

Activity A Answers, p. 65
1. computer game
2. baby boomer
3. eye-opening
4. outreach
5. networking
6. grasslands
7. citizen
8. cross-cultural
9. oversight
10. testing ground

Tip for Success (1 minute)

Have a volunteer read the tip aloud.

B (10 minutes)

1. Preview the instructions and place students into pairs. Ensure that each pair has a dictionary.

2. When students are done, model pronunciation of each word for the class, and have students repeat.

C (10 minutes)

1. Preview the directions and model the activity by completing the first statement as an example.

2. Direct students to complete the activity individually and check answers with a neighbor when done.

3. Check answers as a class.

> **Activity C Answers, p. 65**
> 1. eye-opening
> 2. grasslands
> 3. volunteer tourism
> 4. testing ground
> 5. cross-cultural
> 6. a baby boomer

 For additional practice with compound words, have students visit *Q Online Practice.*

▶ *Listening and Speaking 5, page 66*

SPEAKING

Grammar: Comparative structures
(10 minutes)

1. Present information to students and highlight how the structures are similar with different word forms: *In comparisons, nouns, some adjectives, and some adverbs can use the structure "more __ than."*

2. Check comprehension. Ask students to give additional examples of comparisons. Then ask: *How do you avoid repetition of elements?*

Tip for Success (1 minute)

Have a volunteer read the tip aloud.

Skill Note

Point out to students that when ending a comparative with a possessive noun, the noun that is being possessed can be deleted from the second element. For example, in the sentence "Jose's science project is more interactive than Tim's," "science project," or a pronoun, doesn't have to follow "Tim's."

▶ *Listening and Speaking 5, page 67*

A (10 minutes)

1. Direct students to preview the statements and complete the task individually.

2. Put students in pairs to discuss their answers.

3. Call on volunteers to share their ideas.

> **Activity A Answers, p. 67**
> 1. I
> 2. them
> 3. the Sedgwick one
> 4. Tim's
> 5. the flight to Frankfurt
> 6. regular vacations
> 7. my way
> 8. a term in England

Tip for Success (3 minutes)

Ask a volunteer to read the tip aloud. Practice this pronunciation tip with a few examples from Activity A.

B (10 minutes)

1. Place students into pairs and have them preview the instructions and statements.

2. Direct the pairs to complete the activity and discuss their answers with a nearby pair when done.

> **Activity B Answers, p. 67**
> Answers may vary.

 For additional practice with comparative structures, have students visit *Q Online Practice.*

Pronunciation: Intonation with choices (15 minutes)

 CD1, Track 25

1. Present the information to students, playing the audio at the highlighted points.

2. Check comprehension. Ask: *What's the difference between a choice statement and a choice question? When do we use falling intonation?*

▶ *Listening and Speaking 5, page 69*

A (10 minutes)

 CD1, Track 26

1. Preview the instructions and the statements. Have students predict the intonation pattern for the first statement and discuss their predictions as a class.

2. Pair students to complete the activity.

3. Play the audio clip so students can check their answers and make any corrections needed.

Activity A Answers, p. 69

1. Who paid for the travel expenses, the students or the school?

2. Would you choose to initiate a new project or work on an old one?

3. I'm not sure if I prefer Cambridge, Oxford, Harvard, or Stanford.

4. Which adjective is best, *compelling*, *liberating*, or *enticing*?

5. You have your choice of staying in a tent, a home, or a hotel.

6. Can everyone go on a volunteer vacation, including children, teens, and adults?

Tip for Success (1 minute)

Ask a volunteer to read the tip aloud.

B (10 minutes)

1. Direct students to fill out the questions individually.

2. Pair students and direct them to take turns asking and answering each other's questions.

Activity B Answers, p. 69
Answers will vary.

 For additional practice with intonation with choices, have students visit *Q Online Practice*.

▶ *Listening and Speaking 5, page 70*

Speaking Skill: Discussing preferences and alternatives (10 minutes)

1. Ask volunteers to read the skill information.

2. Check comprehension: *What expressions do we use to talk about past preferences? Current preferences? What are some examples of both?*

A (10 minutes)

1. Pair students. Ask them to preview the instructions and the activity, and ask questions if they have any. Then direct them to complete the activity.

2. When pairs are done, discuss student answers as a class. Correct as necessary.

Activity A Answers, pp. 70–71
2. B: They choose to take small groups of travelers.
3. B: He would prefer to have many more participants.
4. B: The professor hopes to show them that they can be scientists too.
5. B: I think the kids would rather learn at the nature preserve.
6. B: Some children might choose to study there.
7. B: I think his preference is for more visitors.

▶ *Listening and Speaking 5, page 71*

B (10–15 minutes)

1. Place students into groups of three and direct them to create the role-play. Offer support as needed.

2. Choose a few groups to present their role-plays to the rest of the class. Ask those listening to take notes on the choices listed in the role-plays.

 For additional practice with discussing preferences and alternatives, have students visit *Q Online Practice*.

Q Unit Assignment: Plan and present a school trip

Unit Question (5 minutes)

Refer students back to the ideas they discussed at the beginning of the unit about where work, education, and fun overlap. Cue students if necessary by asking specific questions about the content of the unit: *How did people combine work and fun in this unit?*

Learning Outcome

1. Tie the Unit Assignment to the unit learning outcome. Say: *The outcome for this unit is to present a school vacation plan. This Unit Assignment is going to let you show your skill in presenting a school vacation plan.*

2. Explain that you are going to use a rubric similar to their self-assessment rubric on p. 74 to grade their Unit Assignment. You can also share a copy of the Unit Assignment Rubric (on p. 12 of this *Teacher's Handbook*) with students.

Consider the Ideas

A (10 minutes)

Direct students to read the two provided texts individually.

▶ *Listening and Speaking 5, page 72*

B (5–10 minutes)

When done, pair students to compare the two texts.

C (10 minutes)

Discuss answers to the question as a class.

Prepare and Speak

Gather Ideas

A (15 minutes)

1. Place students in groups of three to complete the activity.

2. Preview the activity and direct students to brainstorm ideas and select one trip to present on.

▶ *Listening and Speaking 5, page 73*

Organize Ideas

B (25 minutes)

1. Preview the directions to the activity and model how to fill in the chart using a sample trip.

2. Have students work in their same groups of three from the previous activity to complete this activity.

Speak

C (25–30 minutes)

1. Give students time to practice their parts individually and as a group.

2. When groups are ready, call on students to give their presentations to the class.

3. Use the Unit Assignment Rubric on p. 33 of this *Teacher's Handbook* to score each student's presentation.

4. Alternatively, divide the class into large groups and have students give their presentations to their group. Have listeners complete the Unit Assignment Rubric.

▶ *Listening and Speaking 5, page 74*

D (5 minutes)

Have the class vote on their favorite trip from the options they heard. Ask students to defend their choices with reasons.

Alternative Unit Assignments

Assign or have students choose one of these assignments to do instead of, or in addition to, the Unit Assignment.

1. Describe a unique work, education, or vacation experience you have had and explain whether it was memorable because you learned a lot, had fun, worked hard, or all three.

2. Present some ways environmental organizations could make volunteer vacations more attractive to potential tourists.

 For an additional unit assignment, have students visit *Q Online Practice.*

Check and Reflect

Check

A (10 minutes)

1. Direct students to read and complete the self-assessment rubric.

2. Ask for a show of hands for how many students gave all or mostly *yes* answers.

3. Congratulate them on their success. Remind them that they can refer to the rubric before they begin the Unit Assignment so they can focus on the skills needed to do well. Have students discuss with a partner what they can improve.

Reflect

B (5 minutes)

Ask students to consider the questions in pairs or groups of three. When the conversations have tapered off, ask: *What did you find difficult about persuading your classmates?*

▶ *Listening and Speaking 5, page 75*

Track Your Success (5 minutes)

1. Have students circle the words they have learned in this unit. Suggest that students go back through the unit to review any words they have forgotten.

2. Have students check the skills they have mastered. If students need more practice to feel confident about their proficiency in a skill, point out the page numbers and encourage them to review.

3. Read the Learning Outcome aloud. Ask studens if they feel that the have met the outcome.

Unit Assignment Rubric

Student name: _____

Date: _____

20 points = Presentation element was completely successful (at least 90% of the time).
15 points = Presentation element was mostly successful (at least 70% of the time).
10 points = Presentation element was partially successful (at least 50% of the time).
 0 points = Presentation element was not successful.

Plan and Present a School Trip	20 points	15 points	10 points	0 points
Student spoke clearly and at a good speed about the topic.				
Student used comparative structures correctly.				
Student used at least five vocabulary words from the unit.				
Student used intonation correctly for questions and choices.				
Student discussed preferences and alternatives.				

Total points: _____

Comments:

LISTENING • recognizing appositives that explain **VOCABULARY** • word forms and suffixes **GRAMMAR** • relative clauses **PRONUNCIATION** • stress shifts with suffixes **SPEAKING** • clarifying information	**LEARNING OUTCOME** Deliver a presentation that describes and gives examples of how optical illusions are used and discusses implications of their use.

▶ *Listening and Speaking 5, page 77*

Preview the Unit

Learning Outcome

1. Ask for a volunteer to read the unit skills, then the unit learning outcome.

2. Explain: *This is what you are expected to be able to do by the unit's end. The learning outcome explains how you are going to be evaluated. With this outcome in mind, you should focus on learning these skills (Listening, Vocabulary, Grammar, Pronunciation, Speaking) that will support your goal of "delivering a presentation on optical illusions." This can also help you act as mentors in the classroom to help the other students meet this outcome.*

A (10 minutes)

1. Ask: *Do you know what a mirage is? Have you ever seen one? What causes a mirage?*

2. Put students in pairs or small groups to discuss the first question.

3. Call on volunteers to share their ideas with the class. Ask questions: *In what situations have your eyes played tricks on you? What did you see?*

4. Focus students' attention on the photo. Have a volunteer describe the photo to the class. Read the question aloud. Place students into pairs and have them answer the question. Have the class write some of their answers on the board.

Activity A Answers, p. 77
Possible answers:
1. Yes, I've had this experience. Some artists purposely create paintings or pictures that can be interpreted in different ways.
2. Just as the picture of the miniature city shows a trick of perception, laser light shows aren't always what they seem. You think you're looking at 3D images when you're really just looking at points of light.

B (10–15 minutes)

1. Introduce the Unit Question, "How can the eyes deceive the mind?" Ask related questions to help students prepare for answering the more abstract Unit Question: *Have you ever tried to deceive people with a costume or other device to change your physical appearance? How did they react?*

2. Put students in small groups and give each group a piece of poster paper and a marker.

3. Read the Unit Question aloud. Give students a minute to silently consider their answers to the question. Tell students to pass the paper and the marker around the group. Direct each group member to write a different answer to the question. Encourage them to help one another.

4. Ask each group to choose a reporter to read the answers to the class. Point out similarities and differences among the answers. If answers from different groups are similar, make a group list that incorporates all of the answers. Post the list to refer to later in the unit.

Activity B Answers, p. 77
Possible answers: The eyes can deceive the mind by seeing only what the person wants to see or expects to see. Sometimes when we move quickly, objects blur causing us to see different things than what is actually there.

The Q Classroom (5 minutes)
🔊 CD2, Track 2

1. Play The Q Classroom. Use the example from the audio to help students continue the conversation. Ask: *How did the students answer the question? Do you agree or disagree with their ideas? Why?*

2. Say: *In the audio, Felix mentions that we use visual deception all the time. Do you agree? How do you, or people you know, use visual deception?*

Listening and Speaking 5, page 78

C (5–10 minutes)

Place students into pairs and have them consider the photos and discuss their purpose.

D (5 minutes)

1. Ask pairs to consider the examples of visual deception, checking off those they have tried.

2. As a class, discuss other examples students created.

MULTILEVEL OPTION

Have lower-level students think of more examples of visual deception. Direct them to write their examples on the board. Then ask higher-level students to discuss how each is an example of visual deception. Ask the class if anyone has tried to use these new examples before to deceive someone.

E (10 minutes)

1. Place students into groups of four to answer the questions. Offer support as needed.

2. Discuss answers as a class.

3. Refer back to students' answers to the Unit Question by asking: *How does your conversation about these questions help you answer the Unit Question, "How can the eyes deceive the mind?"*

Listening and Speaking 5, page 79

LISTENING

LISTENING 1: Wild Survivors

VOCABULARY (15 minutes)

1. Preview the bolded vocabulary terms.

2. Pair students and direct them to read through the text and place the vocabulary items next to the correct definitions.

3. When students are done, check answers as a class.

MULTILEVEL OPTION

Pair lower- and higher-level students together. Tell the pairs to write an additional sample sentence for each expression. Have volunteers write one of their sentences on the board. Correct the sentences with the whole class, focusing on the use of the expression rather than other grammatical issues.

Vocabulary Answers, pp. 79–80

1. predator   2. camouflage
3. survival   4. prey
5. adapt   6. mimic
7. resemble   8. mature
9. elaborate   10. virtually
11. obvious   12. infinite

 For additional practice with the vocabulary, have students visit *Q Online Practice*.

Listening and Speaking 5, page 80

PREVIEW LISTENING 1 (5 minutes)

1. Direct students to look at the photos. Ask: *Have you seen these animals before? Where? How are they deceiving other animals?*

2. Pair students and have them answer the questions. Tell students they should review their answers after the Listening.

Tip for Success (1 minute)

Ask a volunteer to read the tip aloud.

Listening 1 Background Note

According to scientists, over time, animals have adapted to their environments. Some have changed the color of their fur, the thickness of their skin, the size of their feet, the smells they produce, and even the way they process oxygen. But why? Mainly adaptation occurs because animals' habitats change. Over time, the animals' genetic information then changes so they are better suited for the habitat. Unfortunately, animals that are not able to adapt to new changes in the environment die, leaving the survivors to pass along their genes.

Teaching Note

Students may find the following words or phrases difficult.

well suited: (phr.) right or appropriate for something

speckled: (adj.) covered with small marks or spots

hatch: (v.) to come out of an egg (a young bird, fish, insect, etc.)

nectar: (n.) a sweet liquid that is produced by flowers and collected by bees for honey

▶ *Listening and Speaking 5, page 81*

LISTEN FOR MAIN IDEAS (10 minutes)

🔊 CD2, Track 3

1. Preview the instructions and model how to fill in the chart.

2. Play the audio and have students complete the activity individually.

3. Place students into pairs and ask them to compare their answers. Then check answers as a class.

> **Listen for Main Ideas Answers, p. 81**
> Answers will vary but may include:
> 1. **Type of camouflage:** Feathers
> 2. **Animal:** Oak tree moth caterpillars
> 3. **Type of camouflage:** Body shape, color;
>   **How it works:** Matches the Asian orchid so predators can't find it
> 4. **Animal:** Desert snake;
>   **How it works:** Almost invisible in the sand
> 5. **Animal:** Caribbean flounder;
>   **Type of camouflage:** Body color same as ocean floor;
>   **How it works:** Hides in the seabed

LISTEN FOR DETAILS (10 minutes)

🔊 CD2, Track 4

1. Direct students to read the statements before they listen again.

2. As you play the audio, have students listen and circle the best answer.

3. Have students compare answers with a partner.

4. Replay the audio so that partners can check their answers.

5. Go over the answers with the class.

> **Listen for Details Answers, pp. 81–82**
> 1. North America 2. feet
> 3. only 4. under leaves
> 5. movement 6. birds
> 7. flower 8. lizard
> 9. eyes 10. behaviors

 For additional practice with listening comprehension, have students visit *Q Online Practice.*

▶ *Listening and Speaking 5, page 82*

Q WHAT DO YOU THINK? (10 minutes)

1. Ask students to read the questions and reflect on their answers.

2. Seat students in small groups and assign roles: a group leader to make sure everyone contributes, a note-taker to record the group's ideas, a reporter to share the group's ideas with the class, and a timekeeper to watch the clock.

3. Give students five minutes to discuss the questions. Call time if conversations are winding down. Allow them an extra minute or two if necessary.

4. Call on each group's reporter to share ideas with the class.

MULTILEVEL OPTION

Pair lower- and higher-level students together and have them answer the questions together.

> **What Do You Think? Answers, p. 82**
> Possible answers:
> 1. Predators can use camouflage to hide from prey until they attack.
> 2. People can dress like and even act like others to blend in. An advantage is that people might not notice you and might leave you alone. A disadvantage is that you'll look just like everyone else and might lose some individuality.
> 3. A person might want to stand out if they don't want to change parts of themselves they are comfortable with—even if those parts, like the way they dress, might stand out.

Learning Outcome

Use the learning outcome to frame the purpose and relevance of Listening 1. Ask: *What did you learn from Listening 1 that prepares you to deliver a presentation on optical illusions?*

Listening Skill: Recognizing appositives that explain (5 minutes)

🔊 CD2, Track 5

1. Present the information on recognizing appositives.

2. Ask students to listen to the audio and guess which expression is the appositive, based on the intonation used in each sentence.

3. Check comprehension by asking questions: *What is an appositive? How are appositives usually highlighted in a written sentence?* (with commas)

A (10 minutes)

 CD2, Track 6

1. Ask a volunteer to read the directions aloud.

2. Play the audio and have students match the appositives to the word or idea it explains.

3. Direct students to compare answers with a partner and check answers as a class.

> **Listening Skill A Answers, p. 83**
> **1.** f **2.** a **3.** g **4.** d **5.** b

 For additional practice with recognizing appositives, have students visit *Q Online Practice*.

▶ *Listening and Speaking 5, page 83*
LISTENING 2: Magic and the Mind

VOCABULARY (15 minutes)

1. Write bolded vocabulary terms on the board and model pronunciation. Then ask students to identify the meaning of words they already know.

2. Put students in groups of two or three and have them complete the activity.

3. When groups have finished working, elicit answers. Correct as necessary.

> **Vocabulary Answers, pp. 83–84**
> **1.** a; **2.** a; **3.** a; **4.** b; **5.** b; **6.** b;
> **7.** b; **8.** a; **9.** a; **10.** b; **11.** a; **12.** b

Tip for Success (1 minute)

Read the tip aloud and stress that knowing the prepositions that go with a word will help students learn how to use new words faster.

 For additional practice with the vocabulary, have students visit *Q Online Practice*.

▶ *Listening and Speaking 5, page 85*
PREVIEW LISTENING 2 (5 minutes)

1. Direct students' attention to the photos and ask: *What profession do you think the man in the photo is part of? How does that profession relate to the learning outcome for this unit?*

2. Preview the Listening title and ask students to predict what topics they'll hear about in the Listening. Tell students they should review their answers after the Listening.

Listening 2 Background Note

Magicians have been making a living off of twisting people's perceptions of reality for generations. Their tricks have been handed down across the generations, and modern magicians are required to take an oath not to reveal the secrets of their trades. Some of their trademark feats, such as levitating heavy objects, often test scientific beliefs of the audience. In fact, throughout history, magicians' "tricks" have challenged what we know about science, religion, and recently, psychology, as we try to explain our physical world.

LISTEN FOR MAIN IDEAS (10 minutes)

 CD2, Track 7

1. Preview the directions. Probe for previous knowledge by asking: *Do you know any of these words? What do you think they mean?*

2. Play the audio and have students complete the activity individually.

3. Place students into pairs so they can explain the terms to their partner. Emphasize that they should use their own words to restate the ideas.

> **Listen for Main Ideas Answers, p. 85**
> Answers will vary but may include:
> **1.** Misdirection: Distracting the audience's attention somewhere else, so that they don't see the trick.
> **2.** Illusions: People see what they expect to see; magicians manipulate people to believe they are seeing something that isn't there.
> **3.** Forcing: Influencing someone's choice in a way that they're not aware of.

Tip for Success (3 minutes)

Ask a volunteer to read the tip aloud. Ask: *What discourse markers do you use or often hear?*

▶ *Listening and Speaking 5, page 86*
LISTEN FOR DETAILS (10 minutes)

 CD2, Track 8

1. Direct students to read the questions before they listen again.

2. As you play the audio, have students listen and select the best answer.

3. Have students compare answers with a partner.

4. Replay the audio so that partners can check their answers.

5. Go over the answers with the class.

For additional practice with listening
comprehension, have students visit *Q Online Practice*.

▶ *Listening and Speaking 5, page 87*

WHAT DO YOU THINK?

A (10 minutes)

1. Ask students to read the questions and reflect on
   their answers.

2. Seat students in small groups and assign roles: a
   group leader to make sure everyone contributes,
   a note-taker to record the group's ideas, a reporter
   to share the group's ideas with the class, and a
   timekeeper to watch the clock.

3. Give students five minutes to discuss the
   questions. Call time if conversations are winding
   down. Allow them an extra minute or two
   if necessary.

4. Call on each group's reporter to share ideas with
   the class.

Activity A Answers, p. 87
Possible answers:
1. Dr. Kuhn would say we cannot perceive everything
   that is happening in our environment, so our eyes
   might not be telling our mind all the information
   that it needs to know.
2. Dr. Kuhn the psychologist is more interested in
   studying how magic works because he feels it can
   give him insight into how people perceive the world
   around them.

Tip for Success (1 minute)

Read the tip aloud.

Critical Q: Expansion Activity

Extend (10 minutes)

1. Read the Critical Thinking Tip from page 87.
2. Ask students: *Why is the ability to extend your
   knowledge important?*
3. Provide students with the following examples
   and ask students to consider how knowledge
   from the first field can help people in the second
   field: (1) Math & Geography, (2) Art & Politics, and
   (3) Science & Literature.

---

4. Ask students to come up with more pairings that
   on the surface might not appear complementary
   and then to discuss how information from one
   field could be extended to the other.

B (5 minutes)

1. Have students continue working in their small
   groups to discuss the questions in Activity B. Tell
   them to choose a new leader, recorder, reporter,
   and timekeeper.

2. Call on the new reporter to share the group's
   answers to the questions.

Learning Outcome

Use the learning outcome to frame the purpose and
relevance of Listenings 1 and 2 and the Critical Q
activity. Ask: *What did you learn from Listenings 1
and 2 and the Critical Q that prepares you to deliver a
presentation on optical illusions?*

▶ *Listening and Speaking 5, page 88*

Vocabulary Skill: Word forms and suffixes (10 minutes)

1. Present the information on suffixes to the class.

2. Check comprehension: *What is a suffix? What are
   some suffixes that indicate a noun? An adjective? An
   adverb? How can learning suffixes help you?*

Skill Note

Suffixes, at a glance, can allow students to identify
the part of speech of a word. Students familiar with
common suffixes can recognize words in new forms
that are part of a word family. Many academic word
lists provide word families. Encourage students to
become familiar with what words mean when they
feature a different suffix if the root is the same.

EXPANSION ACTIVITY: Working with Suffixes (20 minutes)

1. Ask students to look at the list of suffixes in the
   Vocabulary Skill box on page 88. Place students
   into pairs and give them three minutes to make as
   many words as they can, using the suffixes.

2. After three minutes, ask pairs, one at a time, to
   read one word from their list. If other pairs have
   that same word, all pairs need to cross the word
   off their list. The winner will have the most
   words still remaining.

► *Listening and Speaking 5, page 89*

A (10 minutes)

1. Pair students and have them preview the instructions and chart. Remind students to use a dictionary to check the word forms they list.

2. Go over the answers with the class.

> **Activity A Answers, p. 89**
> **Nouns:** 3. deceit, deceiver, deception; 5.difference; 6. individual; 7. maturity; 8. prey, predator; 9. technician, technique
> **Verbs:** 2. adapt; 4. decorate; 6. individualize; 7. mature; 8. prey; 9. X
> **Adjectives:** 2. adaptive; 3. deceptive; 4. decorative; 5. different; 6. individual
> **Adverb:** 2. adaptively; 3. deceptively; 4. decoratively; 5. differently; 7. maturely; 8. predatorily; 9. technically

---

MULTILEVEL OPTION

Pair lower- and higher-level students together and have them choose six to eight words from Activity A to create a dialog about deception. Ask volunteers to share their dialogues with the class.

B (10 minutes)

1. Preview the instructions and ask students to complete the activity individually.

2. Check answers as a class.

> **Activity B Answers, p. 89**
> **1.** imagination
> **2.** predator
> **3.** deceive
> **4.** individual
> **5.** adaptive
> **6.** mature

 For additional practice with suffixes, have students visit *Q Online Practice.*

► *Listening and Speaking 5, page 90*

SPEAKING

Grammar: Relative clauses (15 minutes)

1. Present the information to the class. Provide or elicit more examples as needed.

2. Check comprehension. Ask: *How are relative clauses similar to appositives? What relative pronouns can we use? What's the difference between subject and object relative clauses?*

Skill Note

Relative clauses follow and add extra information to a noun phrase. Because relative clauses convey a lot of information, learners of English sometimes end a statement at the end of the clause. For example, a learner might say or write, "The man who is coming to dinner." However, it is important to note that this is not a complete sentence as there is no main verb linked to the subject. Another common error is that some learners use a pronoun, such as *he* or *she,* instead of a relative pronoun. Provide students with enough practice to help them avoid these common errors.

► *Listening and Speaking 5, page 92*

A (10 minutes)

 CD2, Track 9

1. Direct students to preview the directions.

2. Play the audio.

3. Put students in pairs to discuss the answers that they circled.

4. Call on volunteers to explain their answers.

> **Activity A Answers, p. 92**
> **1.** b **2.** c **3.** b **4.** a **5.** c **6.** c

B (10 minutes)

1. Preview the directions. Model the activity by completing the first statement together.

2. Direct students to complete the activity.

3. Pair students to read their sentences and listen for subject-verb agreement or pronoun problems.

4. When students are done, choose volunteers to write their answers on the board. Correct as needed.

> **Activity B Answers, p. 92**
> Answers will vary but may include:
> **1.** David Copperfield, whose real name is David Seth Kotkin, is one of the most famous modern magicians.
> **2.** Cyril Takayama, who was born in Hollywood, has performed for orphans in Thailand./Cyril Takayama, who has performed for orphans in Thailand, was born in Hollywood.
> **3.** Color change is the most common form of camouflage, which I didn't know before I took this class.
> **4.** Stage illusions that use exotic animals such as tigers are often performed for large audiences./ Stage illusions that are performed for large audiences often use exotic animals such as tigers.

5. Some creatures hide in the sand or in the seaweed, where they can't be seen because of their coloring./ Some creatures that hide in the sand or in the seaweed can't be seen because of their coloring.

6. Houdini, who became famous as an escape artist, really wanted to be a magician.

 For additional practice with relative clauses, have students visit *Q Online Practice*.

Listening and Speaking 5, page 93
Pronunciation: Stress shifts with suffixes (5–10 minutes)

CD2, Track 10

1. Present the information to the class and play the audio at the appropriate time.

2. Check comprehension by asking questions: *What are some rules that you can follow when deciding where to place stress on words with suffixes?*

Listening and Speaking 5, page 94
A (5 minutes)

CD2, Track 11

1. Preview the directions and have students complete the activity.

2. Play the audio for students to check their work

3. Check answers as a class, saying each word aloud.

Activity A Answers, p. 94
a. manipulate   b. manipulation
a. alternate   b. alternative
a. deceive   b. deception
a. image   b. imaginary
a. technique   b. technically
a. mystery   b. mysterious
a. popular   b. popularity
a. psychology   b. psychological
a. terrify   b. terrific
a. visual   b. visualize

B (5 minutes)

1. Place students into pairs and ask them to read each sentence, paying attention to word stress.

2. Ask volunteers to read each sentence aloud. Correct as needed.

 For additional practice with stress shifts with suffixes, have students visit *Q Online Practice*.

Listening and Speaking 5, page 95
Speaking Skill: Clarifying information (5 minutes)

CD2, Track 12

1. Present the information to the class and play the audio at the appropriate time.

2. Check comprehension: *What phrases can you use to restate a speaker's point? To ask the speaker to rephrase something that has been said? How do you rephrase a difficult idea without being asked?*

A (10 minutes)

1. Pair students and have them complete the task.

2. When the conversations taper off, choose a pair to present the conversation to the class. Model pronunciation of difficult words.

Activity A Answers, pp. 95–96
Answers will vary but may include:
1. what do you mean by
2. Could you give an example
3. That is/In other words,
4. So are you saying that/So do you mean that
5. just to clarify

Listening and Speaking 5, page 96
B (20–25 minutes)

1. Preview the instructions and offer ideas on how to construct a role-play from the listed scenario and incorporate one or more of the concepts.

2. Place students into pairs and direct them to create and practice their role-play.

3. Have pairs present their role-plays to the class.

 For additional practice with clarifying information, have students visit *Q Online Practice*.

Unit Assignment: Give a group presentation on the uses of illusions

Unit Question (5 minutes)

Refer students back to the ideas they discussed at the beginning of the unit about how the eyes can deceive the mind. Cue students if necessary by asking specific questions about the content of the unit: *Why would animals need to deceive other animals? Why would people need or want to deceive other people?*

Learning Outcome

1. Tie the Unit Assignment to the unit learning outcome. Say: *The outcome for this unit is to deliver a presentation on optical illusions. This Unit Assignment is going to let you show your skill in delivering a presentation on optical illusions.*

2. Explain that you are going to use a rubric similar to their self-assessment rubric on p. 98 to grade their Unit Assignment. You can also share a copy of the Unit Assignment Rubric (on p. 43 of this *Teacher's Handbook*) with students.

Consider the Ideas (20 minutes)

1. Preview the instructions and directs students to consider the slides in groups of three.

2. As students discuss the questions, circulate around the room and take note of interesting answers.

3. Discuss answers as a class, highlighting some of the interesting answers you heard.

▶ *Listening and Speaking 5, page 97*

Prepare and Speak

Gather Ideas

A (20–25 minutes)

1. Have students work in their same groups of three to complete the activity.

2. Discuss students' ideas as a class.

21ST CENTURY SKILLS

To aid in thinking creatively, people need to brainstorm in teams and encourage each other to explore new ideas. Provide further practice with brainstorming by having students generate as many ideas as they can without judging others' ideas or dominating the discussion. Provide students with several questions, such as "What illusions might young people experience?" or "Why do you think people are so drawn to illusions?" and have students brainstorm answers. Ensure that all students get an opportunity to speak and are encouraged.

Organize Ideas

B (15–20 minutes)

1. Preview the instructions and have students work in their same groups. Provide support as necessary.

2. Remind students to use note cards when preparing for their presentation. Review note card skills from Unit 1 as needed.

▶ *Listening and Speaking 5, page 98*

Speak

C (15–25 minutes)

1. Call on groups to present their ideas to the class.

2. Use the Unit Assignment Rubric on p. 43 of this *Teacher's Handbook* to score each student's presentation.

3. Alternatively, divide the class into large groups and have students give their presentations to their group. Have listeners complete the Unit Assignment Rubric.

Alternative Unit Assignments

Assign or have students choose one of these assignments to do instead of, or in addition to, the Unit Assignment.

1. Talk about the differences and similarities in the ways animals and humans can be deceived.

2. Narrate a story that includes an example of deception, such as a magic trick, a lie, cheating, an optical illusion, or camouflage that you have used, observed, or been a victim of.

3. Discuss the ways that deception can have both positive and negative effects on people.

 For an additional unit assignment, have students visit *Q Online Practice*.

Check and Reflect

Check

A (10 minutes)

1. Direct students to read and complete the self-assessment rubric.

2. Ask for a show of hands for how many students gave all or mostly *yes* answers.

3. Congratulate them on their success. Remind them that they can refer to the rubric before they begin the Unit Assignment so they can focus on the skills needed to do well. Have students discuss with a partner what they can improve.

B (5-10 minutes)

Ask students to consider the questions in pairs. When the conversations have tapered off, ask: *Was it difficult to think of examples for this outcome? Why or why not? What's a good technique for thinking of a lot of examples?*

▶ *Listening and Speaking 5, page 99*

Track Your Success (5 minutes)

1. Have students circle the words they have learned in this unit. Suggest that students go back through the unit to review any words they have forgotten.

2. Have students check the skills they have mastered. If students need more practice to feel confident about their proficiency in a skill, point out the page numbers and encourage them to review.

3. Read the Learning Outcome aloud. Ask students if they feel that they have met the outcome.

Unit Assignment Rubric

Student name: _____

Date: _____

20 points = Presentation element was completely successful (at least 90% of the time).
15 points = Presentation element was mostly successful (at least 70% of the time).
10 points = Presentation element was partially successful (at least 50% of the time).
 0 points = Presentation element was not successful.

Give a Group Presentation on the Uses of Illusions	20 points	15 points	10 points	0 points
Group members spoke easily about the topic and at a good speed.				
Group members used relative clauses correctly.				
Group members used at least five vocabulary items from the unit.				
Group members used correct syllable stress with various word forms.				
Group members offered clarifications of their ideas at least twice.				

Total points: _____

Comments:

UNIT 5

Unit QUESTION

What does it mean to be a global citizen?

Global Cooperation

LISTENING • organizing notes with a T-chart
VOCABULARY • collocations
GRAMMAR • reported speech
PRONUNCIATION • linking with final consonants
SPEAKING • citing sources

LEARNING OUTCOME

Identify and report on aspects of a global problem.

▶ *Listening and Speaking 5, page 101*

Preview the Unit

Learning Outcome

1. Ask for a volunteer to read the unit skills, then the unit learning outcome.

2. Explain: *This is what you are expected to be able to do by the unit's end. The learning outcome explains how you are going to be evaluated. With this outcome in mind, you should focus on learning these skills (Listening, Vocabulary, Grammar, Pronunciation, Speaking) that will support your goal of "identifying and reporting on aspects of a global problem." This can also help you act as mentors in the classroom to help the other students meet this outcome.*

A (10 minutes)

1. Ask the class: *What does it mean to be a citizen? What are you a citizen of?*

2. Put students in pairs or small groups to discuss the first two questions.

3. Call on volunteers to share their ideas with the class. Ask questions: *What can or should people do about issues such as hunger or poverty? How can people in one part of the world help people in another part of the world? Should they help?*

4. Focus students' attention on the photo. Have a volunteer describe the photo to the class. Read the question aloud. Ask: *What do you think the people in this picture are doing? Where do you think this food is going?*

Activity A Answers, p. 101
Possible answers:
1. Short-term problems get a lot of attention because they have the potential to lead to long-term problems.

2. I have done work similar to what's represented in the picture. I worked with a group that collected food and brought it to a location where we cooked and served the food for families without food.

B (10 minutes)

1. Introduce the Unit Question, "What does it mean to be a global citizen?" Ask questions to help students prepare for answering the more abstract Unit Question: *What are some issues that affect citizens of every country? How can people work together to solve these problems? What are some organizations that help people all over the world?*

2. Label four pieces of poster paper *(Donate Money to Global Causes, Become Informed About Different Parts of the World, Volunteer in Different Countries, and Work to Make Your Own Country Better)* and place them in the corners of the room.

3. Ask students to read and consider the Unit Question, and then to stand in the corner next to the poster that best represents their answer.

4. Direct the groups in each corner to talk amongst themselves about the reasons for their answer. Tell them to choose a secretary to record the answers on the poster paper.

5. Call on volunteers from each corner to share their opinions with the class.

6. Leave the posters up for students to refer back to at the end of the unit.

Activity B Answers, p. 101
Possible answers:
Being a global citizen means to help people in other parts of the world. When people donate their time and their resources to make other people's lives better, they are being global citizens.

---

44 Unit 5

The Q Classroom (5 minutes)

CD2, Track 13

1. Play The Q Classroom. Use the example from the audio to help students continue the conversation. Ask: *How did the students answer the question? Do you agree or disagree with their ideas? Why?*

2. Say: *In the audio, Felix mentions that businesses need to act responsibly. What does he mean by that? What can a business do to act responsibly?*

▶ *Listening and Speaking 5, page 102*

C (10 minutes)

1. Preview the instructions and model how to complete the activity by soliciting ideas about what problem is represented in the first photo.

2. Place students into pairs to complete the activity.

3. Discuss answers as a class, including the problems students brainstormed.

MULTILEVEL OPTION

Pair lower- and higher-level students to brainstorm problems the world faces today and possible solutions. Ask the higher-level students to record their ideas.

D (10 minutes)

1. Preview the instructions and explain what an NGO is—an organization that is not affiliated with a government.

2. Place students into groups of four and direct them to complete the chart.

3. Share answers as a class and invite the class to debate their classmates' choices.

EXPANSION ACTIVITY: Create an NGO (20 minutes)

1. Review what an NGO is and ask: *Do you know of any NGOs?* If so, ask: *What do they do?* Tell students they are going to create an NGO.

2. Divide students into groups of three and direct them to invent an NGO. Have them identify the problem it would help to solve, how it could help, and where it would work. Make sure students give the NGO a name as well.

3. Have groups present their NGO to the class, and encourage the class to ask follow-up questions.

▶ *Listening and Speaking 5, page 103*

LISTENING

LISTENING 1: The Campaign to Humanize the Coffee Trade

VOCABULARY (10 minutes)

1. Say each bolded vocabulary item three times, modeling pronunciation, and ask students to repeat.

2. Choose a volunteer to read each statement. Then, as a class, match each vocabulary item with its corresponding definition.

MULTILEVEL OPTION

Pair lower- and higher-level students together to read through the statements and match the vocabulary items with the definitions. Check answers as a class.

Vocabulary Answers, pp. 103–104

a. speculation	**b.** transform	**c.** roughly
d. guarantee	**e.** commodity	**f.** intermediary
g. processor	**h.** devise	**i.** activist
j. afford	**k.** massive	**l.** co-op

 For additional practice with the vocabulary, have students visit *Q Online Practice.*

▶ *Listening and Speaking 5, page 104*

PREVIEW LISTENING 1 (5 minutes)

1. Direct students to look at the photo. Ask: *What's in the basket that the person in the photo is holding?*

2. Direct students to read and predict what the speaker will say. Tell students they should review their answers after the Listening.

Listening 1 Background Note

The Fair Trade movement began as a way to pay farmers living wages. Their products are labeled Fair Trade. The organizations that label products as Fair Trade refer to a set of principles known as FINE—an acronym of four international fair trade groups. In the early 2000s, FINE members agreed that Fair Trade should work toward sustainable development in the areas where Free Trade products are grown. This includes paying the growers of these products a higher percentage of the money made from the fruits of their labor. As you'll soon hear, coffee that sells for up to $9 per pound in the U.S. provides the farmers who grew it only $0.50 per pound. FINE guidelines and Fair Trade practices seek to give the growers a more equitable share of the profits.

Teaching Note

Students may find the following words or phrases difficult.

lug: (v.) to carry or drag something heavy, with a lot of effort

shack: (n.) a small building, usually made of wood or metal, that has not been built well

plank: (n.) a long narrow flat piece of wood that is used for making floors, walls, etc.

derisively: (adv.) unkindly

puzzled: (adj.) unable to understand something or the reason for something

siphon off: (phr.) to remove money from one place and move it to another, especially dishonestly or illegally

▶ *Listening and Speaking 5, page 105*

LISTEN FOR MAIN IDEAS (10 minutes)

 CD2, Track 14

1. Preview the instructions and the topics as a class.

2. Play the audio and have students complete the activity individually.

3. Place students into pairs and have them read their statements. Check as a class.

> **Listen for Main Ideas Answers, p. 105**
> Answers will vary but may include:
> 1. The coffee farmers live in poverty, and even though they work hard, they live in shacks without water or electricity.
> 2. The coffee farmers are poor because they have to sell to middlemen who do not pay the farmers enough to live on.
> 3. The Fair Trade system is designed to make sure that the coffee farmers get a fair wage. In order for it to work, consumers have to pay more for Fair Trade products.

LISTEN FOR DETAILS (10 minutes)

 CD2, Track 15

A (10 minutes)

1. Direct students to preview the statements before listening to the audio.

2. As you play the audio, have students listen and check the true statements.

3. Have students compare answers with a partner.

4. Replay the audio so that partners can check their answers.

5. Go over answers with the class.

> **Listen for Details Answers A, p. 105**
> Check (✓) 2, 5, 6, and 8.

▶ *Listening and Speaking 5, page 106*

B (10 minutes)

1. Preview the instructions and read the first item.

2. Direct students to complete the activity.

3. Play the audio and have partners check their answers. Review answers as a class.

> **Listen for Details Answers B, p. 106**
> **5.** a coffee shop
> **1.** a coyote, or middleman
> **2.** a processor
> **4.** a roaster
> **6.** the consumer
> **3.** an exporter

web+ For additional practice with listening comprehension, have students visit *Q Online Practice*.

21ST CENTURY SKILLS

One aspect of critical thinking is figuring out how parts of a system work together–just as students did when piecing together the order of events in the coffee trade. If people understand how the pieces move together, then they'll be able to help new participants in the group work efficiently toward the group's goals. Put students into groups of three and have them brainstorm the steps in another process. After groups have identified the steps, have them take turns explaining the process to another group.

❓ WHAT DO YOU THINK? (10 minutes)

1. Ask students to read the questions and reflect on their answers.

2. Seat students in small groups and assign roles: a group leader to make sure everyone contributes, a note-taker to record the group's ideas, a reporter to share the group's ideas with the class, and a timekeeper to watch the clock.

3. Give students five minutes to discuss the questions. Call time if conversations are winding down. Allow them an extra minute or two if necessary.

4. Call on each group's reporter to share ideas with the class.

MULTILEVEL OPTION

Place students in groups of two. Pair one higher-level student with one lower-level student. Have the higher-level student interview the lower-level student using the questions from "What Do You Think?" and record their answers to share with the class.

What Do You Think? Answers, p. 106
Possible answers:
1. I am willing to pay more for products that are traded fairly, but sometimes I don't have enough money to do it.
2. Consumers would have to commit to buying only coffee that was labeled as Fair Trade.
3. Buyers and sellers should work together to determine a fair price. If one person in the system, consumers or farmers, decided on a price, it might be too low or too high because each would be looking after their own interests.

Learning Outcome

Use the learning outcome to frame the purpose and relevance of Listening 1. Ask: *What did you learn from Listening 1 that prepares you to identify and report on aspects of a global problem?*

▶ *Listening and Speaking 5, page 107*

Listening Skill: Organizing notes with a T-chart (10 minutes)

🔊 CD2, Track 16

1. Present the information in the Listening Skill box. Play the highlighted audio at the appropriate time.

2. Check comprehension by asking questions: *How can T-charts help you organize notes? What common patterns can be easily categorized in a T-chart? What can you do if you miss information?*

▶ *Listening and Speaking 5, page 108*

Listening Skill Activity (10 minutes)

🔊 CD2, Track 17

1. Ask a volunteer to read the instructions.

2. Play the audio and direct students to fill in the problems and solutions as they listen.

3. Pair students to compare answers; then check answers as a class.

Listening Skill Activity Answers, p. 108
Answers will vary but may include:
1. Problem: poverty
   Solution: buy Fair Trade products
2. Problem: water crisis
   Solution: World Water Organization, protect water
3. Problem: environmental problems like pollution
   Solution: Leonardo DiCaprio Foundation, expand public awareness, grassroots campaign to end use of plastic bags
4. Problem: The Disaster Relief Group is new and small, so it can be hard to raise money for this organization.
   Solution: They are improving outreach and communications through their website.

 For additional practice with organizing notes with a T-chart, have students visit *Q Online Practice*.

Critical Q: Expansion Activity

Identify (20 minutes)

1. Read the Critical Thinking Tip from page 108.
2. Place students into groups of three and have them brainstorm three problems they see in their city or country. Then direct students to come up with a solution for each problem.
3. Ask groups to develop a small presentation about their ideas. Presentations should not simply be a list of problems and solutions. Students should also explain why they see those things as problems and why they think their solutions could work.
4. As each group presents their ideas, students should take notes on the problems and solutions discussed so they can ask follow-up questions.

LISTENING 2: The UN Global Compact

Tip for Success (1 minute)

Direct a volunteer to read the tip aloud. Review what a collocation is.

VOCABULARY (20–25 minutes)

1. Read the directions. Check comprehension by reading the first sentence together and selecting the correct definition of the bolded collocation.

2. Put students into groups of three and assign roles: one reader, one decider, and one writer. The reader reads the sentence, the group discusses the correct answer, the decider makes the final decision, and the writer writes the answer.

3. Check answers as a class, and then choose a few collocations to have the class write model sentences with. Have pairs create one new sentence for each collocation.

4. Direct a few volunteers to write one of their sentences on the board. Correct the sentences as a class if necessary.

> **Vocabulary Answers, pp. 108–110**
> **a.** labor standards
> **b.** social impact
> **c.** emerging economy
> **d.** confidence of investors
> **e.** household expenditures
> **f.** accounting practices
> **g.** ethical goods
> **h.** intangible assets
> **i.** sustainable market
> **j.** exploit
> **k.** proactive
> **l.** core strategies

 For additional practice with the vocabulary, have students visit *Q Online Practice*.

 Listening and Speaking 5, page 110

PREVIEW LISTENING 2 (5 minutes)

1. Direct students' attention to the photo and ask: *What is the United Nations?*

2. Ask: *What is a compact? What kind of compact might the UN create?*

3. Direct students to check the issues they expect to hear about in the Listening. Tell students they should review their answers after the Listening.

Listening 2 Background Note

The UN Global Compact (UNGC) holds ten principles as core to its missions. The principles are divided among four categories: Human Rights, Labor, Environment, and Anti-Corruption. A selection of principles, as presented by the UNGC, are as follows:

Principle 1: Businesses should support and respect the protection of internationally proclaimed human rights.

Principle 4: Businesses should uphold the elimination of all forms of forced and compulsory labor.

Principle 7: Businesses should support a precautionary approach to environmental challenges.

Principle 10: Businesses should work against corruption in all its forms, including extortion and bribery.

Teaching Note

Students may find the following words or phrases difficult.

incur: (v.) if you incur costs, you have to pay for them

byword: (n.) a word or phrase that is well known or often used

scrutiny: (n.) a careful and thorough examination

assets: (n.) things of value, especially property, which can be used or sold to pay debts

plummet: (v.) to fall suddenly and quickly from a high level or position

tattered: (adj.) in bad condition

on the flip side: (phr.) on the other hand; conversely

▶ *Listening and Speaking 5, page 111*

LISTEN FOR MAIN IDEAS (10 minutes)

))) CD2, Track 18

1. Preview the instructions and each of the statements.

2. Direct students to discuss with a partner which answer they think will complete each statement.

3. Play the audio and have students complete the activity individually.

4. Pair students to have them compare answers. Then discuss answers as a class.

> **Listen for Main Ideas Answers, p. 111**
> **1.** b **2.** a **3.** a **4.** b **5.** a **6.** b

LISTEN FOR DETAILS (10 minutes)

🔊 CD2, Track 19

1. Direct students to preview the details before they listen again.
2. As you play the audio, have students listen and place the numbers into the T-chart.
3. Have students compare answers with a partner.
4. Replay the audio so that partners can check their answers.
5. Go over the answers with the class. Provide pronunciation modeling for any numbers the class had difficulty hearing.

Listen for Details Answers, p. 112
1. 1989 **2.** 11 million **3.** one trillion **4.** 2000
5. 10 **6.** 70 percent **7.** $90 **8.** 90 percent
9. 38 **10.** 120

 For additional practice with listening comprehension, have students visit *Q Online Practice*.

Q WHAT DO YOU THINK?

A (10 minutes)

1. Ask students to read the questions and reflect on their answers.
2. Seat students in small groups and assign roles: a group leader to make sure everyone contributes, a note-taker to record the group's ideas, a reporter to share the group's ideas with the class, and a timekeeper to watch the clock.
3. Give students five minutes to discuss the questions. Call time if conversations are winding down. Allow them an extra minute or two if necessary.
4. Call on each group's reporter to share ideas with the class.

Activity A Answers, p. 112
Possible answers:
1. The Global Compact should force businesses to address their impact on the environment.
2. I think businesses are motivated by profit because some consumers will only do business with Compact members.
3. In my experience, businesses have tried to become better integrated with their communities in order to help solve problems in the area and improve their image.

B (5 minutes)

1. Have students continue working in their small groups to discuss the questions in Activity B. Tell them to choose a new leader, recorder, reporter, and timekeeper.
2. Call on the new reporter to share the group's answers to the questions.

Learning Outcome

Use the learning outcome to frame the purpose and relevance of Listenings 1 and 2 and the Critical Q activity. Ask: *What did you learn from Listenings 1 and 2 and the Critical Q that prepares you to identify and report on aspects of a global problem?*

Vocabulary Skill: Collocations (10 minutes)

1. Present the information on collocations.
2. Check comprehension: *What is a collocation? Why might a thesaurus not be helpful when constructing collocations?*

Skill Note

If your classroom has ready access to the Internet, there are online linguistic corpora you can use to discover which words typically collocate with words that you might be studying in your class. Search on Google for "American Corpus" and you'll find a searchable corpus on American English that will allow you to discover which words collocate with any word you want to search for. You can find collocation patterns with any part of speech by using the "pos list" function. Try it out for yourself!

A (10 minutes)

1. Direct students to complete the activity individually. Offer support as necessary.
2. Ask students to compare their answers with a partner.
3. Go over the answers with the class.

Activity A Answers, pp. 113–114
1. human rights **2.** final draft
3. prices rose **4.** up and down
5. short supply of **6.** disaster relief
7. do some research **8.** Emerging markets
9. coffee shop **10.** climate change

Read the tip aloud. If you have Internet access in the classroom, have students apply this search technique to the answer choices from Activity A.

▶ *Listening and Speaking 5, page 114*

B (10 minutes)

1. Preview the instructions and place students into pairs. Ensure that each pair has a dictionary.

2. Model the activity by showing how to fill in the ellipses with the word in the first item.

3. Check answers as a class.

> **Activity B Answers, p. 114**
> **1.** a, c **2.** a, b **3.** b, c **4.** b, c **5.** a, c **6.** a, b

C (10 minutes)

1. Preview the directions and model the activity by making a statement with the first collocation.

2. Choose volunteers to create sentences with a few of the collocations.

3. Direct pairs to then write sentences for each collocation and compare sentences with another pair when done.

4. Choose volunteers to write a sentence on the board. Correct as necessary.

 For additional practice with collocations, have students visit Q Online Practice.

▶ *Listening and Speaking 5, page 115*

SPEAKING

Grammar: Reported speech
(20 minutes)

1. Read the first paragraph in the Grammar box to students.

2. Check comprehension by asking questions: *What is reported speech? Why do we use it? What is important to do when using reported speech?*

3. Then, present each example of reported speech from the chart in turn, eliciting questions from students about each as you move forward.

Skill Note

Tell students that using reported speech can help them avoid plagiarism, which is when you use someone else's words or ideas in your work as if the ideas were your own. By using reported speech, students can attribute ideas to the person whose idea it originally was. Emphasize the importance of this skill in academic writing.

▶ *Listening and Speaking 5, page 116*

A (10 minutes)

1. Direct students to preview the statements and complete the task with a partner.

2. Put students in groups of four to discuss and compare their answers.

3. Call on volunteers to share their ideas with the class. Correct as needed.

> **Activity A Answers, p. 116**
> **1.** The farmer stated that growing coffee was a lot of work, and sometimes they couldn't even cover their costs.
> **2.** Deborah Amos asked the audience if they thought about the farmers who grew the coffee.
> **3.** Georg Kell said that the Global Compact had initially started off with a moral core.
> **4.** Ban Ki-Moon pointed out that together we can achieve a new face of globalization.
> **5.** Dan Zwerdling said that those farmers were the poorest and most powerless part of the global coffee trade.
> **6.** Dan Zwerdling said that the Fair Trade network can't raise all the money that farmers need just by cutting out middlemen, but consumers have to help too.

B (10 minutes)

1. Place students into groups of five and have them preview the instructions and examples.

2. Choose a few volunteers to come to the front of the room to model the activity with you.

3. Direct the groups to complete the activity. Circulate around the room to offer support as needed.

 For additional practice with reported speech, have students visit *Q Online Practice.*

▶ *Listening and Speaking 5, page 117*

Pronunciation: Linking with final consonants (15 minutes)

🔊 CD2, Track 20

1. Present the information to students, playing the audio at the highlighted point.

2. Check comprehension by asking questions: *What is a final consonant? What does the text say about thought groups? What are the three principles of linking? Can you provide an example of each?*

3. Practice this linking by pairing students and asking them to take turns reading the examples.

▶ *Listening and Speaking 5, page 118*

A (10 minutes)

🔊 CD2, Track 21

1. Preview the instructions and the phrases. Model how to use each symbol by referring back to the skill box on the previous page. Ask the class which symbol they should use with "an economist." (The "sounds are joined" symbol.)

2. Direct students to complete the activity individually, and then check answers and practice pronunciation with a partner when done.

3. Choose volunteers to write the answers (with the symbols) on the board and explain their answers.

4. Play the audio and have students mimic the pronunciation.

Activity A Answers, p. 118
1. an economist
2. growing coffee
3. special label
4. stuck in poverty
5. can't cover costs
6. basic commodity
7. household expenditure
8. global expansion
9. climate change
10. environmental issues

B (10 minutes)

1. Direct students to mark the linked places individually.

2. Have students compare their answers with a partner, and then check answers as a class.

3. Pair students and direct them to ask and answer the questions, focusing on linking final consonants.

Activity B Answers, p. 118
1. What time is the conference on the global economy?
2. What kind of help does a refugee camp provide?
3. How can countries demonstrate international unity?
4. What are some ways to help earthquake victims?
5. How can companies promise to reduce their environmental impact?
6. What are some nonprofit organizations that collect food donations for the hungry?
7. What are some ways you take care of the people in your community?
8. How might an economist describe fair trade?

 For additional practice with linking with final consonants, have students visit *Q Online Practice*.

▶ *Listening and Speaking 5, page 119*

Speaking Skill: Citing sources (10 minutes)

1. Ask volunteers to read the information on citing sources to the class, alternating reading paragraphs.

2. Check comprehension: *What benefits can citing sources give you? In what ways can you cite information when speaking? How does this skill complement reported speech? When do we use a present perfect verb form to cite sources? What are some common phrases for citing sources?*

A (10 minutes)

1. Preview the instructions and the activity. Direct students to complete the activity individually.

2. Have pairs compare their answers. Then discuss student answers as a class. Correct as necessary.

Activity A Answers, pp. 119–120

Answers will vary but may include:

1. According to Wikipedia,
2. In 2005, the BBC news reported that
3. Rose Tran Bach Yen, an orphanage director in Vietnam, reports that
4. In a McKinsey survey published in 2007, results showed that
5. When accepting his Academy Award in February 2007, Al Gore told his fellow Americans that
6. Pediatrician Susan Shepherd explained in her January 30, 2008 *New York Times* article that

▶ *Listening and Speaking 5, page 120*

Tip for Success (1 minute)

1. Read the tip aloud before beginning Activity B.
2. Emphasize that variation is a key part of language use—not everyone says everything in the same ways.

B (10–15 minutes)

1. Preview the instructions and model the activity by eliciting an example of how information can be cited from the first description.
2. Place students into pairs and direct them to complete the task. Offer support as needed.
3. Choose a few pairs to present their citations to the rest of the class.

 For additional practice with citing sources, have students visit *Q Online Practice*.

Unit Assignment: Report on a global problem

Unit Question (5 minutes)

Refer students back to the ideas they discussed at the beginning of the unit about what it means to be a global citizen. Cue students if necessary by asking specific questions about the content of the unit: *In what ways did people cooperate together to solve global issues? How are citizens taking or not taking responsibility for the world?*

Learning Outcome

1. Tie the Unit Assignment to the unit learning outcome. Say: *The outcome for this unit is to identify and report on aspects of a global problem. This Unit Assignment is going to let you explore that learning outcome by reporting on a global problem.*

2. Explain that you are going to use a rubric similar to their self-assessment rubric on p. 122 to grade their Unit Assignment. You can also share a copy of the Unit Assignment Rubric (on p. 54 of this *Teacher's Handbook*) with students.

Consider the Ideas (15 minutes)

1. Place students into groups of four.
2. Direct the groups to consider the flyer and discuss the questions which follow it.
3. As a class, review some of the group's answers. Ask follow-up questions as needed (e.g., *What in the flyer gave you that impression?*).

▶ *Listening and Speaking 5, page 121*

Prepare and Speak

Gather Ideas

A (15 minutes)

1. Place students into new groups of four.
2. Preview the activity and direct groups to brainstorm a list of global problems discussed in the unit.
3. When groups have settled on topics, direct them to fill out the chart. Provide support as needed.

▶ *Listening and Speaking 5, page 122*

Organize Ideas

Tip for Success (1 minute)

1. Ask students to read the tip silently.
2. Ask students to share examples or situations of when they have heard points numbered.

B (25 minutes)

1. Preview the instructions and the roles for the group members. Direct group members to decide which student will fill which role.
2. Explain to students where they can find sources of information beyond their textbook (e.g., the Internet, the library, knowledgeable peers, etc.).
3. Direct students to plan and practice their presentations. Review note card skills if necessary.

Speak

C (25 minutes)

1. Direct groups to give their presentations to the class.

2. Use the Unit Assignment Rubric on p. 54 of this *Teacher's Handbook* to score each student's presentation.

3. Alternatively, divide the class into large groups and have students give their presentations to their group. Have listeners complete the Unit Assignment Rubric.

Alternative Unit Assignments

Assign or have students choose one of these assignments to do instead of, or in addition to, the Unit Assignment.

1. Summarize the ways some businesses are trying to decrease their negative image by "going green" or advertising the ways they are decreasing their ecological footprint (the demands their company puts on the Earth's ecosystems).

2. Explain how natural disasters bring people from different countries together, including celebrities, to provide humanitarian aid.

3. Present some ways that the public could put pressure on global businesses to uphold the principles of the Global Compact.

 For an additional unit assignment, have students visit *Q Online Practice*.

Check and Reflect

Check

A (10 minutes)

1. Direct students to read and complete the self-assessment rubric.

2. Ask for a show of hands for how many students gave all or mostly *yes* answers.

3. Congratulate them on their success. Remind them that they can refer to the rubric before they begin the Unit Assignment so they can focus on the skills needed to do well. Have students discuss with a partner what they can improve.

Reflect

B (5–10 minutes)

Ask students to consider the questions in pairs or groups of three. When the conversations have tapered off, ask: *How did working in a group help you identify and report on global problems?*

▶ *Listening and Speaking 5, page 123*

Track Your Success (5 minutes)

1. Have students circle the words they have learned in this unit. Suggest that students go back through the unit to review any words they have forgotten.

2. Have students check the skills they have mastered. If students need more practice to feel confident about their proficiency in a skill, point out the page numbers and encourage them to review.

3. Read the Learning Outcome aloud. Ask students if they feel that they have met the outcome.

Unit Assignment Rubric

Student name: _____

Date: _____

20 points = Presentation element was completely successful (at least 90% of the time).
15 points = Presentation element was mostly successful (at least 70% of the time).
10 points = Presentation element was partially successful (at least 50% of the time).
 0 points = Presentation element was not successful.

Report on a Global Problem	20 points	15 points	10 points	0 points
Student spoke clearly and at a good speed about the topic.				
Student used at least five vocabulary words and collocations from the unit.				
Student used reported speech.				
Student linked final sounds in his or her speech.				
Student cited sources appropriately.				

Total points: _____

Comments:

Unit QUESTION
How do you make a space your own?

Personal Space

LISTENING • recognizing organizational cues
VOCABULARY • words with multiple meanings
GRAMMAR • conditionals
PRONUNCIATION • thought groups
SPEAKING • giving advice

LEARNING OUTCOME

Role-play a talk show focused on identifying and solving conflicts centered on issues of personal space.

▶ *Listening and Speaking 5, page 125*
Preview the Unit

Learning Outcome

1. Ask for a volunteer to read the unit skills, then the unit learning outcome.

2. Explain: *This is what you are expected to be able to do by the unit's end. The learning outcome explains how you are going to be evaluated. With this outcome in mind, you should focus on learning these skills (Listening, Vocabulary, Grammar, Pronunciation, Speaking) that will support your goal of "role-playing a talk show focused on identifying and solving conflicts centered on issues of personal space." This can also help you act as mentors in the classroom to help the other students meet this outcome.*

A (15 minutes)

1. Ask the class: *How many of you have your own space at your house?* Of those who raised their hands, ask: *What kinds of things do you like to do in your own space? How do you decorate your own space?* Then tell students a little bit about your own space (in the classroom, at home, etc.).

2. Put students in pairs or small groups to discuss the first two questions.

3. Call on volunteers to share their ideas with the class. Ask questions: *Do people stay out of your space? If you have a sibling or roommate, how is your space different than his or hers? Why do you think people personalize their space differently?*

4. Focus students' attention on the photo. Have a volunteer describe the photo to the class. Read the question aloud. Ask: *What can you say about the personality of the people who live in this house? What from the photo informs your ideas?*

Activity A Answers, p. 125
Possible answers:
1. My bedroom is my own space, and I try to keep people out of it. Because I keep people away from my space and my stuff, they know that I consider that area mine.
2. I think adults personalize their space with furniture while children use toys and games to decorate their areas.
3. I believe the people who live in this house have made the space their own because they have painted the house in a unique way.

B (10 minutes)

1. Introduce the Unit Question, "How do you make a space your own?" Ask related questions to help students prepare for answering the more abstract Unit Question: *Why is it important for you to have your own space?*

2. Tell students: *Let's start off our discussion by listing the ways in which we make a space our own.* Seat them in small groups and direct them to pass around a paper as quickly as they can, with each group member adding one item to the list. Tell them they have two minutes to make the lists, and they should write as many ideas as possible.

3. Call time and ask a reporter from each group to read the list aloud.

4. Use items from the list as a springboard for discussion. For example: *How do people individualize their personal spaces?*

Activity B Answers, p. 125
Possible answers:
I make a space my own by hanging up pictures of people that are important to me. By listening to music I like, I'm able to transform any space into my own. Any place I'm in for long is cluttered with coffee cups, notebooks, books—all of the things I use.

The Q Classroom (5 minutes)
CD2, Track 22

1. Play The Q Classroom. Use the example from the audio to help students continue the conversation. Ask: *How did the students answer the question? Do you agree or disagree with their ideas? Why?*

2. Say: *Like some of you, Felix notes that music can transform a space into his own. Why do you think music can be an important part of transforming a space into one's own?*

▶ *Listening and Speaking 5, page 126*

C (10 minutes)

1. Ask students to look over the pictures and answer the question individually. Direct them to share their answers with a nearby partner when done.

2. Discuss answers as a class. Ask students to support their ideas with details from the pictures.

D (5–10 minutes)

1. Place students into groups of four and preview the instructions to the activity. Model by describing your own space and explaining how it reflects you.

2. Direct students to complete the activity. When done, choose a few volunteers to share their descriptions with the class.

MULTILEVEL OPTION

Pair lower-level students with higher-level students. Have the lower-level student describe his or her personal space and the higher-level student ask questions to determine what the lower-level student's personal space says about him or her (e.g., *Because your space has so many books, do you prefer to be alone?*). Have the higher-level students share information about their partners with the class.

▶ *Listening and Speaking 5, page 127*

LISTENING

LISTENING 1: Environmental Psychology

VOCABULARY (15 minutes)

1. Model pronunciation of the bolded vocabulary words. Have students repeat.

2. Probe for prior knowledge by asking students if they have seen any of these vocabulary words before. If so, ask what they think the words mean.

3. Put students in groups of three, and have them complete the activity.

4. Ask volunteers to read their definition match for the first item. If the answer differs, elicit a correction from the class. Continue with the rest of the definitions, correcting as needed.

MULTILEVEL OPTION

Pair lower- and higher-level students together, and have them create a short dialog using several of the vocabulary words. Direct the higher-level students to make corrections to the writing as needed. Circulate around the room and answer questions as necessary. Choose a pair or two to present their dialogs.

Vocabulary Answers, pp. 127–128
1. b   2. a   3. a   4. b   5. c   6. a
7. c   8. c   9. a   10. c   11. b   12. b

 For additional practice with the vocabulary, have students visit *Q Online Practice*.

▶ *Listening and Speaking 5, page 129*

PREVIEW LISTENING 1 (5 minutes)

1. Direct students to look at the photo. Ask: *Why do you think the brain in this photo is different colors? Do different parts of the brain process different types of information?*

2. Have a volunteer read the directions aloud, and direct students to answer the question individually.

3. Pair students and have them share their answer. Tell students they should review their answer after the Listening.

Listening 1 Background Note

Your idea of personal space isn't just a preference. Small parts of the brain, called "amygdalae," help regulate fear and emotion. They're the part of the brain that also help people know when close is too close when standing next to other people. In a study with a woman whose amygdalae were damaged, personal space was not an issue. She was asked to stand as close to the researcher as was comfortable for her, and she ended up standing nose-to-nose with the researcher—which was likely uncomfortable for the researcher! So next time you feel you need a little more space, remember to thank your amygdalae.

Tip for Success (1 minute)

Ask a student to read the tip aloud. Suggest to students to keep a vocabulary journal.

LISTEN FOR MAIN IDEAS (25 minutes)

 CD2, Track 23

A (15 minutes)

1. Preview the instructions for the activity and the terms in the outline.
2. Play the audio and have students complete the activity individually.
3. When done, place students into groups of three and have them review their answers. Replay the audio as needed if groups are missing answers.
4. Have a group read their completed outline and correct as needed.

> **Listen for Main Ideas A Answers, pp. 129–130**
> Answers will vary but may include:
> I.A: The study of the interrelationship between human behaviors and environments
> I.B.1: gender; 2: eye contact; 3: privacy
> II: territorial
> II.A.2: Adjacent
> II.B.1: jacket; 2: books
> II.D: plates; restaurants
> III.A: less; big city
> III.B: more; small town
> IV.A.2: Offices

Critical Q: Expansion Activity

Outline (10 Minutes)

1. Read the Critical Thinking Tip from page 129.
2. Have students look at their completed outline from Listen for Main Ideas A in pairs. Ask them to recreate the lecture by presenting it to one another using just the outline.
3. Choose one or two volunteers to present the lecture to the class. Then, ask the class to explain how using an outline can help a speaker organize his or her thoughts.

▶ *Listening and Speaking 5, page 130*

B (10 minutes)

1. Direct students to answer the questions individually, using their outlines.

2. When done, ask students to compare their answers with a partner.
3. Check answers as a class.

> **Listen for Main Ideas B Answers, pp. 130-131**
> Suggested answers:
> 1. Environmental psychology is the study of human behavior and its response to environments.
> 2. Males and females display different territorial behavior. Males compete and females affiliate.
> 3. When we want more privacy, we avoid eye contact; when we have a personal connection with people, we feel more comfortable making eye contact.
> 4. A lack of privacy can make people feel stressed or threatened.

▶ *Listening and Speaking 5, page 131*

LISTEN FOR DETAILS (10 minutes)

 CD2, Track 24

1. Direct students to read the statements before they listen again.
2. As you play the audio, have students listen and write *T* (true) or *F* (false) next to each statement.
3. Have students compare answers with a partner.
4. Replay the audio so that partners can check their answers.
5. Go over the answers with the class.

> **Listen for Details Answers, p. 131**
> **1.** F **2.** F **3.** T **4.** T **5.** F
> **6.** T **7.** F **8.** F **9.** T **10.** F

 For additional practice with listening comprehension, have students visit *Q Online Practice*.

▶ *Listening and Speaking 5, page 132*

WHAT DO YOU THINK? (10 minutes)

1. Ask students to read the questions and reflect on their answers.
2. Seat students in small groups and assign roles: a group leader to make sure everyone contributes, a note-taker to record the group's ideas, a reporter to share the group's ideas with the class, and a timekeeper to watch the clock.
3. Give students five minutes to discuss the questions. Call time if conversations are winding down. Allow them an extra minute or two if necessary.
4. Call on each group's reporter to share ideas with the class.

As a class, make a possible answer bank that lower-level students can use as they answer the questions in this activity (e.g., *I never touch a hot plate at a restaurant* or *I don't believe males and females have different reactions to space because we're all human.*)

What Do You Think? Answers, p. 132
Possible answers:
1. I always sit in the same seat in the classroom. I always touch my plate at a restaurant—just to see how hot it is.
2. Yes, the examples convince me, but now I'm trying to think of why males and females act differently. Maybe society conditions men and women differently?
3. I think that in cultures where people live in big spaces, people's idea of personal space is bigger while in cultures where people live close together, personal space is smaller.

Learning Outcome

Use the learning outcome to frame the purpose and relevance of Listening 1. Ask: *What did you learn from Listening 1 that prepares you to role-play a talk show?*

Listening Skill: Recognizing organizational cues (15 minutes)

1. Present the information on the Listening Skill.
2. Check comprehension by asking questions: *Why are organizational cues useful? What kinds of cues signal importance? Evidence? Shifting topics? Which of these cues have you used or heard used?*

▶ *Listening and Speaking 5, page 133*

A (10 minutes)
CD2, Track 25

1. Ask a student to read the instructions aloud.
2. Play the audio and have students list the cues individually.
3. Place students into pairs, refer them back to the Listening Skill box on page 132, and have them discuss why Dr. Craig used each cue.
4. Discuss answers as a class.

Listening Skill A Answers, p. 133
1. In addition; signals additional support or evidence
2. for example; signals examples or illustrations
3. In fact; signals emphasis
4. Equally important; signals importance
5. that is; signals an example or illustration
6. In short; signals a conclusion or summary

B (5–10 minutes)
CD2, Track 26

1. Preview the instructions.
2. Play the audio and direct students to select the correct ending for each sentence.
3. Check answers as a class.

Listening Skill B Answers, p. 133
1. b 2. a 3. b 4. a 5. a 6. b

EXPANSION ACTIVITY: Organizing Your Thoughts
(20 minutes)

1. Tell students that listening for organizational cues will help them understand what they hear. Emphasize that the best way for students to be able to hear the cues is to produce them. Ask students to create a short presentation on their personal space requirements using these cues.
2. Place students into pairs and direct them to prepare a three- to five-minute presentation on their personal space. They should use at least five organizational cues in their presentations.
3. Have students practice their presentations. Then direct the audience to take notes on which cues they hear during each final presentation.
4. After each presentation, ask the class to report on the cues that they heard.

 For additional practice with recognizing organizational cues, have students visit *Q Online Practice.*

▶ *Listening and Speaking 5, page 134*

LISTENING 2: What Your Stuff Says About You

VOCABULARY (25 minutes)

1. Ask students to study the spelling of the vocabulary words for three minutes. Then give an impromptu spelling quiz.

2. When the quiz is concluded, have students check their answers on pages 134–135.

3. Then ask students to complete the vocabulary activity individually.

4. Check answers as a class.

Vocabulary Answers, pp. 134–135
1. modify
2. propose
3. introvert
4. clues
5. clarify
6. profile
7. tentatively
8. traits
9. extrovert
10. domain
11. crucial
12. framework

 For additional practice with the vocabulary, have students visit *Q Online Practice*.

▶ *Listening and Speaking 5, page 135*

PREVIEW LISTENING 2 (5 minutes)

1. Direct students' attention to the photo and ask: *What does a person's messy desk tell you about his or her personality?*

2. Pair students and have them read through the information and question.

3. Direct students to discuss their answer to the question.

4. Tell students they should review their answer after the Listening.

Listening 2 Background Note

Dr. Sam Gosling bills himself as a "personality/social psychologist." His primary interest is in how people take clues from the environment to mold their own personalities and understand other people's personalities. He finds that people typically fit into five broad personality traits: extroversion, agreeableness, conscientiousness, neuroticism, and openness. His work also extends into the animal world, on what constructs personality traits in animals.

Teaching Note

Students may find the following words or phrases difficult.

cork board: (n.) a bulletin board; a place for posting papers, photos, announcements, etc.

disingenuous: (adj.) not sincere

pull the wool over somebody's eyes: (idiom) to try to trick somebody

construe: (v.) to understand the meaning of a word, a sentence, or action in a particular way

etiquette: (n.) the formal rules of correct or polite behavior in society

rigorous: (adj.) done carefully and with a lot of attention to detail

LISTEN FOR MAIN IDEAS (15 minutes)

 CD2, Track 27

1. Preview the questions with the class.

2. Pair students and have them predict what they think the answer to each question might be.

3. Play the audio and have students complete the activity individually.

4. Direct students to compare their answers with a partner, and ask students to compare the correct answers with their predicted answers.

5. Check answers as a class.

Listen for Main Ideas Answers, p. 135
1. He snoops around offices, cars, bedrooms, and bathrooms.
2. No. He thinks we sometimes make mistakes by jumping to conclusions or relying on stereotypes. The "stuff" is just one part of what we should analyze.
3. You add up all the pieces—your belongings, physical places, and virtual places that you inhabit—to get a general picture of someone's personality.

▶ *Listening and Speaking 5, page 136*

LISTEN FOR DETAILS (10 minutes)

CD2, Track 28

1. Direct students to read the statements before they listen again.

2. As you play the audio, have students listen and complete the statements.

3. Have students compare answers with a partner.

4. Replay the audio so that partners can check their answers.

5. Go over the answers with the class.

Listen for Details Answers, p. 136
1. his radio operator's license; family pictures
2. how the objects are arranged
3. offices, music collections, rooms in houses, websites
4. oral environments are music, CDs; virtual environments are Web pages or Facebook pages
5. extroverts and introverts
6. impressions people got from handshakes
7. come to the wrong conclusion because we base our view on just one part of the person, on one clue
8. sentimental

 For additional practice with listening comprehension, have students visit *Q Online Practice*.

WHAT DO YOU THINK?

A (15 minutes)
1. Ask students to read the questions and reflect on their answers.
2. Seat students in small groups and assign roles: a group leader to make sure everyone contributes, a note-taker to record the group's ideas, a reporter to share the group's ideas with the class, and a timekeeper to watch the clock.
3. Give students five minutes to discuss the questions. Call time if conversations are winding down. Allow them an extra minute or two if necessary.
4. Call on each group's reporter to share ideas with the class.

Activity A Answers, p. 136
Possible answers:
1. I do believe that we are natural "snoops" because we are all interested in what other people have. For example, I think it's interesting visiting someone's home. You can see part of them that they might not easily reveal.
2. I think Dr. Gosling would say that we are organized people who are creative because of all the projects that are displayed in our classroom.

▶ *Listening and Speaking 5, page 137*

B (10 minutes)
1. Have students continue working in their small groups to discuss the questions in Activity B. Tell them to choose a new leader, recorder, reporter, and timekeeper.

2. Call on the new reporter to share the group's answers to the questions.

Learning Outcome
Use the learning outcome to frame the purpose and relevance of Listenings 1 and 2 and the Critical Q activity. Ask: *What did you learn from Listenings 1 and 2 and the Critical Q that prepares you to role-play a talk show?*

Vocabulary Skill: Words with multiple meanings (5 minutes)
1. Present the information on the Vocabulary Skill.
2. Check comprehension: *How can the dictionary help you choose the correct definition?*

Skill Note
Many common words in English can have multiple meanings. For example, *get* can mean "to have" as in "I've got the book," or "to understand" as in "I've got the idea," or "to obtain" as in "I'll get the car." Point out words with multiple meanings in context so students learn to recognize their different meanings.

▶ *Listening and Speaking 5, page 138*

A (10 minutes)
1. Pair students and give each pair a dictionary.
2. Preview the directions for the activity, and point out that students will not use all the definitions. Ask students to complete the activity.
3. Go over the answers with the class.

Activity A Answers, pp. 138–139
1. b 2. a 3. f 4. d 5. h
6. i 7. k 8. j 9. o 10. n

▶ *Listening and Speaking 5, page 139*

B (10 minutes)
1. Preview the directions with the class.
2. Model the activity by completing the task for "place" on the board.
3. Have students complete the activity by selecting a different word to look up. Offer support as needed.

Activity B Answers, p. 139
Answers will vary.

C (10 minutes)

Preview the directions with the class, and ask students to work in pairs to complete the task. Circulate around the classroom to offer support.

 For additional practice with words with multiple meanings, have students visit *Q Online Practice*.

▶ *Listening and Speaking 5, page 140*

SPEAKING

Grammar: Conditionals (15 minutes)

1. Present the information on the Grammar Skill. Probe for prior knowledge by asking: *When have you seen or heard this grammar form used before?*

2. Check comprehension by asking questions: *What does the verb tense in a conditional show? What are the three types of conditionals discussed? Can you give an example of each? What do you consider the difference between each conditional?*

Tip for Success (1 minute)

Read the Tip for Success aloud and point out that people often speak differently than they write, especially in informal situations.

Skill Note

Clarify situations where conditionals are used. For example, tell students the present real conditional can be used to decide whether or not a solution to a problem can work (e.g., *If we make houses smaller, we could save fuel used for heating*). The present/future unreal conditional can be used to explain why something likely won't happen (e.g., *If she didn't want people to comment on how messy she is, she would clean her space*). The past unreal conditional can be used to explain why something did not happen (e.g., *If she had wanted to be anonymous, she wouldn't have used her real name*).

A (10 minutes)

1. Direct students to circle the correct conclusion based upon the conditional.

2. Put students in pairs to discuss their answers.

3. Call on volunteers to share their ideas.

> **Activity A Answers, pp. 140–141**
> **1.** b **2.** b **3.** b **4.** b **5.** a **6.** b

▶ *Listening and Speaking 5, page 141*

B (10 minutes)

1. Have a volunteer read the directions to the activity.

2. As a class, brainstorm possible completions of the first statement.

3. Ask students to complete the remainder of the task individually, compare completions with a partner, and check each other's verb forms.

4. Choose volunteers to share their statements with the class. Discuss which conditional has been used.

> **Activity B Answers, p. 141**
> Answers will vary.

 For additional practice with conditionals, have students visit *Q Online Practice*.

▶ *Listening and Speaking 5, page 142*

Pronunciation: Thought groups
(10 minutes)

 CD2, Track 29

1. Probe students' prior knowledge by asking: *What do you think a thought group is?*

2. Present the information on the Pronunciation Skill, playing the audio at the highlighted point.

3. Check comprehension by asking questions: *What is a thought group? How do speakers separate thought groups? What are some strategies to make effective thought groups?*

4. Have students practice reading the thought group patterns listed in the Pronunciation Skill box.

A (15 minutes)
 CD2, Track 30

1. Preview the instructions for the task and model it by reading through the first sentence together.

2. Play the audio and have students complete the task individually.

3. Check answers with a partner.

4. Play the audio a second time, and have students speak along with the audio.

5. Choose a few students to read the text aloud to the class, focusing on separating the thought groups.

Activity A Answers, p. 142

Answers will vary but may include:

Dr. GOSLING: That's right / because it's really important / you know / if I had one wish / one wish in the world / it would be that one clue / told you something / about a person. / If you had a / stuffed teddy on your bed / it meant something / you know. / But the world / is more complicated than that. / So / unfortunately it doesn't work like that / because there are many reasons why we might have / say a stuffed animal on our bed / or something like that. / And so really / you can't use a code book approach / where x means y. / What you have to do / is you have to build up a picture / piece-by-piece / and sometimes you only have a very little piece / and you have to hold your view / very tentatively. / But that will / that will guide your search / for more information.

▶ *Listening and Speaking 5, page 143*

B (15 minutes)

1. Preview the directions, and direct students to complete the task with a partner.

2. Call on volunteers to read sentences and have the class identify the sentence that was read.

Tip for Success (1 minute)

Choose a volunteer to read the tip aloud. Ask: *Why do you think elongating your thought groups will help you sound more fluent?*

 For additional practice with thought groups, have students visit *Q Online Practice*.

Speaking Skill: Giving advice (5 minutes)

1. Probe for previous experience by asking: *What kind of phrases do you use to give advice?*

2. Choose volunteers to read aloud the information in the Speaking Skill box.

3. Check comprehension: *What does the text say is an important conversation skill? Do you agree? Why or why not? What phrases can we use to give advice in the past? What expressions can you use to give advice strongly?*

▶ *Listening and Speaking 5, page 144*

A (15 minutes)

1. Preview the directions to the activity. Model the activity by reading through the example situation.

2. Direct students to complete the task in groups of three. Remind them to use phrases from page 143.

3. Choose a volunteer for each situation and ask them to give their advice to the class.

Tip for Success (1 minute)

1. Read the tip aloud.

2. Write a few more examples of this construction on the board (e.g., *I recommend that you study English every afternoon*).

B (15 minutes)

1. Preview the instructions and brainstorm a few pieces of advice one might give in this situation.

2. Pair students and ask them to complete the role-play.

3. Circulate around the room, listening to, but not interrupting, the role-plays.

4. Choose one or two pairs to present their role-play to larger groups of students (or the whole class).

 For additional practice with giving advice, have students visit *Q Online Practice*.

Unit Assignment: Role-play a talk show

Unit Question (5 minutes)

Refer students back to the ideas they discussed at the beginning of the unit about how people make a space their own. Cue students if necessary by asking specific questions about the content of the unit: *How are space and personality connected? Why should people be mindful of how their personal space looks?*

Learning Outcome

1. Tie the Unit Assignment to the unit learning outcome. Say: *The outcome for this unit is to role-play a talk show focused on identifying and solving conflicts centered on issues of personal space. This Unit Assignment is going to let you show your skill by performing a role-play.*

2. Explain that you are going to use a rubric similar to their self-assessment rubric on p. 146 to grade their Unit Assignment. You can also share a copy of the Unit Assignment Rubric (on p. 65 of this *Teacher's Handbook*) with students.

Consider the Ideas (15 minutes)

CD2, Track 31

1. Place students into groups of three, and preview the instructions and the questions that students will need to answer.

2. Have students predict answers to the first question based on the picture before the audio begins.

3. Play the audio and have students discuss the questions.

4. When done, briefly discuss answers as a class. Ask: *Was your predicted answer to the first question correct?*

Prepare and Speak

Gather Ideas

A (10 minutes)

1. Have students work in their same groups of three to complete the activity.

2. Preview the chart and provide examples of items that might go into each category.

3. Circulate around the room to provide support and model additional items as needed.

4. Once students' charts are completed, place groups together in sets of two (for a total of six students), and ask groups to compare their answers.

▶ *Listening and Speaking 5, page 146*

Organize Ideas

B (25 minutes)

1. Preview the instructions to the activity and the steps they'll need to follow. Ask a student to summarize the steps required for the activity.

2. Have students complete the activity in their same groups of three.

3. Direct students to write their scripts. Circulate around the room to provide support as needed.

21ˢᵀ CENTURY SKILLS

As the world becomes increasingly interconnected, businesses and other organizations value people who are able to work effectively in groups. Working effectively in a group means valuing every group member's contribution and working hard to incorporate all suggestions into a final product. As students continue to work on their role-plays, provide tips for collaborating effectively: (1) Consider each idea provided, (2) ask for clarification, (3) withhold judgment until ideas are explained, and (4) make eye contact and encourage others to speak.

Tip for Success (1 minute)

Ask a student to read the tip aloud and to demonstrate the tip by stressing the key words.

Speak

C (20 minutes)

1. Call on groups to perform their role-plays.

2. Use the Unit Assignment Rubric on p. 65 of this *Teacher's Handbook* to score each student's presentation.

3. Alternatively, divide the class into large groups and have students give their presentations to their group. Have listeners complete the Unit Assignment Rubric.

Alternative Unit Assignments

Assign or have students choose one of these assignments to do instead of, or in addition to, the Unit Assignment.

1. In his book, *Eye To Eye: How People Interact*, Dr. Peter Marsh reports that "A study of American university dormitories shows how personalization of students' space is related to their sense of belonging to the university as a whole," and affects whether they drop out of school or not. Explain why you think this is or is not true.

2. Describe your most personal space. Use the ideas in the recordings to help you explain what your space says about you and what advice the psychologists would give you.

3. Describe where you usually like to sit in a restaurant, movie theater, classroom, and so on, and why.

 For an additional unit assignment, have students visit *Q Online Practice*.

Check and Reflect

Check

A (10 minutes)

1. Direct students to read and complete the self-assessment rubric.

2. Ask for a show of hands for how many students gave all or mostly *yes* answers.

3. Congratulate them on their success. Remind students that they can refer to the rubric before they begin the Unit Assignment so they can focus on the skills needed to do well. Have them discuss with a partner what they can improve.

Reflect

B (5–10 minutes)

Q Ask students to consider the questions in pairs or groups of three. When the conversations have tapered off, ask: *What part of your role-play are you most proud of? Why? Which part of the role-play was the most difficult?*

▶ *Listening and Speaking 5, page 147*

Track Your Success (5 minutes)

1. Have students circle the words they have learned in this unit. Suggest that students go back through the unit to review any words they have forgotten.

2. Have students check the skills they have mastered. If students need more practice to feel confident about their proficiency in a skill, point out the page numbers and encourage them to review.

3. Read the Learning Outcome aloud. Ask students if they feel that they have met the outcome.

Unit Assignment Rubric

Student name: _____

Date: _____

20 points = Presentation element was completely successful (at least 90% of the time).
15 points = Presentation element was mostly successful (at least 70% of the time).
10 points = Presentation element was partially successful (at least 50% of the time).
 0 points = Presentation element was not successful.

Role-Play an Advice Show	20 points	15 points	10 points	0 points
Student spoke clearly and at a good speed about the topic.				
Student used vocabulary with appropriate connotations.				
Student used conditionals correctly.				
Student used at least five vocabulary items from the unit.				
Student used thought groups appropriately.				
Student used language from the unit to give advice.				

Total points: _____

Comments:

Unit QUESTION
Where do new ideas come from?

Alternative Thinking

LISTENING • distinguishing between facts and opinions
VOCABULARY • idioms and informal expressions
GRAMMAR • noun clauses
PRONUNCIATION • conditional modals: Affirmative and negative
SPEAKING • using formal and informal language

LEARNING OUTCOME

Develop a marketing presentation designed to sell a new invention or idea.

▶ *Listening and Speaking 5, page 149*
Preview the Unit

Learning Outcome

1. Ask for a volunteer to read the unit skills, then the unit learning outcome.

2. Explain: *This is what you are expected to be able to do by the unit's end. The learning outcome explains how you are going to be evaluated. With this outcome in mind, you should focus on learning these skills (Listening, Vocabulary, Grammar, Pronunciation, Speaking) that will support your goal of "developing a marketing presentation designed to sell a new invention or idea." This can also help you act as mentors in the classroom to help the other students meet this outcome.*

A (10 minutes)

1. To get students thinking about where new ideas may come from, ask some of the following questions: *When have you created a new idea or a better way to do something? What were you doing at the time?* Have students answer questions in small groups or elicit answers in a class discussion.

2. Put students in pairs or small groups to discuss the first two questions.

3. Call on volunteers to share their ideas with the class. Ask questions: *What are some of the ways you come up with ideas?*

4. Focus students' attention on the photo. Have a volunteer describe the photo to the class. Read the question aloud. Ask: *What are the women in the photo looking at? What's the benefit of posting ideas to a wall?* Elicit or supply vocabulary as needed.

Activity A Answers, p. 149
Answers will vary but may include:
1. I come up with ideas when I'm alone and it's silent, because I need to give my brain room to think.
2. The best inventions in the past ten years have been related to technology, such as faster and smaller computers and easily accessible Internet, which make our lives easier.
3. It seems that the women are mapping out ideas for a new type of cereal.

B (5 minutes)

1. Introduce the Unit Question, "Where do new ideas come from?" Ask related questions to help students prepare for answering the more abstract Unit Question: *What is a new idea? Why do we need to keep coming up with new ideas?*

2. Have students discuss the Unit Question. List their answers (e.g., "when people are alone" or "in medical labs") on the board.

3. Point out that answers to the Unit Question can fall into categories (e.g., from science, from individual thinkers, during problem-solving, etc.). Write a few of these example categories on the board, and give students a minute to silently think of different categories. Invite students to share their answers.

4. Write each category at the top of a sheet of poster paper. Elicit responses to the Unit Question from students that fall into these categories. Make notes under the correct heading. Ask students for help in determining under which categories their answers fall. Post the lists to refer to later in the unit.

Activity B Answers, p. 149
Answers will vary but may include:
I think ordinary people come up with new ideas on a regular basis because they're always looking to improve their lives. New ideas come out of periods of turmoil that force people to think of different ways to live their lives.

The Q Classroom (5 minutes)

🔊 CD3, Track 2

1. Play The Q Classroom. Use the example from the audio to help students continue the conversation. Ask: *How did the students answer the question? Do you agree or disagree with their ideas? Why?*

2. Elicit all the answers the students in the audio have to the Unit Question. Replay the audio, if needed, to catch all of the responses. Discuss any responses that are different from what the class listed.

▶ *Listening and Speaking 5, page 150*

C (10 minutes)

1. Preview the instructions and the survey. Define and model the pronunciation of any new vocabulary.

2. Direct students to complete the survey individually.

3. Place students into groups of three, and direct them to share their survey responses. Ask students to discuss what their answers show about them.

Activity C Answers, p. 150
Answers will vary.

▶ *Listening and Speaking 5, page 151*

LISTENING

LISTENING 1: Alternative Ideas in Medicine

VOCABULARY (10 minutes)

1. Read the directions. Model how to complete the first item. Have students in pairs choose the word that does not have the same meaning for each item.

2. Group pairs into larger groups and have students check and correct answers.

3. Discuss answers as a class.

Vocabulary Answers, pp. 151-152
1. a ; **2.** c; **3.** b; **4.** b; **5.** b; **6.** c;
7. b; **8.** c; **9.** c; **10.** a; **11.** b; **12.** b

 For additional practice with the vocabulary, have students visit *Q Online Practice*.

▶ *Listening and Speaking 5, page 152*

PREVIEW LISTENING 1 (10 minutes)

1. Have a volunteer read the directions aloud.

2. Place students into pairs and have them consider the photos and brainstorm ideas as directed.

3. When done, place pairs into larger groups to share their lists of ideas. Choose a few volunteers to share their lists with the class.

4. Tell students they should review their answers after the Listening.

Preview Listening 1 Answer, p. 152
Answers will vary.

Listening 1 Background Note

Shipping containers are large metal boxes used to send goods around the world. They typically measure 8'x8'x40' and are transported on cargo ships. Once they are unloaded on docks, they are filled again and shipped to a new location. Recently, people have been purchasing these types of containers and making houses out of them.

The American Apitherapy Society (AAS) was founded in 1989, and publishes a journal and a website to advance "apitherapy"—or the use of bees and bee products in therapy. The organization claims that the use of bee products can alleviate symptoms from ailments such as arthritis, joint and muscle pain, and multiple sclerosis. Research continues to be done with bee venom, and the AAS will continue to be at the forefront of studying this type of therapy.

Teaching Note

Students may find the following words or phrases difficult.

novel: (adj.) new; different from anything known before

immunized: (adj.) vaccinated

paramedic: (n.) a person whose job is to help people who are sick or injured, but who is not a doctor or a nurse

midwife: (n.) a person, especially a woman, who is trained to help women give birth to babies

retrofit: (v.) to put a new piece of equipment into a machine that did not have it when it was built

perforated: (adj.) having a series of small holes through it

mainstream: (n.) the people whose ideas and opinions are most accepted

arthritis: (n.) a disease that causes pain and swelling in one or more joints of the body

booster: (n.) a person who gives their support to somebody or something

▶ *Listening and Speaking 5, page 153*

LISTEN FOR MAIN IDEAS (10 minutes)

CD3, Track 3

A (10 minutes)

1. Choose a student to read the instructions aloud.
2. Play the audio. Ask students to complete the activity individually.
3. Direct students to check answers with a partner. Then discuss answers as a class.

> **Listen for Main Ideas A Answers, p. 153**
> Notes in chart will vary. Sample notes:
>
> | | Report 1: Doc-in-a-Box | Report 2: Bee Sting Therapy |
> | --- | --- | --- |
> | 1. Meaning of the term and where it came from | Doctor in a Box; comes from doctor's office in box-shaped shipping containers | medical therapy using bees; comes from *apis* which means bee in Latin + *therapy* |
> | 2. Problem it is trying to solve | finding a way to provide cheap medical services to remote poor villages | trying to cure diseases in a new alternative way and/or relieve pain |

> | 3. Analysis of the solution: Benefits | reasonable price; use old, abandoned shipping containers; easy transport to remote villages | cheap; works according to anecdotal evidence; can be used by people themselves without doctors |
> | --- | --- | --- |
> | 4. Analysis of the solution: Obstacles | expense: the idea is still in early stages; the prototype clinic was expensive ($5,000) but could be built for less money | not a lot of research; not accepted yet by mainstream doctors; people may have trouble accepting the idea |

B (10 minutes)

CD3, Track 3

1. Preview the instructions. Ask a volunteer to restate the directions.
2. Play the audio. Ask students to complete the activity with a partner.
3. Check answers as a class.

> **Listen for Main Ideas B Answers, p. 153**
> **Report 1: Doc-in-a-Box?**
> **1.** Doc-in-a-Box refers to doctors working in a box-shaped office made out of shipping containers.
> **2.** In some remote villages there are no doctors. Doc-in-a-Box clinics can be built cheaply and transported easily.
> **Report 2: Bee Sting Therapy**
> **3.** Using a bee sting to alleviate pain. Something in the bee venom may help release an anti-inflammatory; the bee stings give venom that may change how the body transmits pain signals to the brain.
> **4.** They are excited about its healing powers and the very inexpensive cost of the treatment.
> **Both Reports:**
> **5.** Obstacles include acceptance by the public and funding for research and development.

▶ *Listening and Speaking 5, page 154*

LISTEN FOR DETAILS (10 minutes)

CD3, Track 4

1. Direct students to read the statements before they listen again.

2. As you play the audio, have students identify statements as true or false and correct false items.

3. Have students compare answers with a partner.

4. Replay the audio so that partners can check their answers.

5. Go over the answers with the class.

> **Listen for Details Answers, p. 154**
> **Report 1**
> 1. F: She is a Pulitzer Prize-winning science writer; 2. F: They could offer medical care to poor people even in remote villages because the container could be easily transported; 3. T; 4. F: Clinics would be staffed by local village paramedics and midwives; 5. T
> **Report 2**
> 6. F: She is a beekeeper and acupuncturist; 7. T; 8. F: It uses the venom from the sting of a live bee; 9. F: Use is strong in Asia and Eastern Europe; 10. T

 For additional practice with listening comprehension, have students visit *Q Online Practice*.

WHAT DO YOU THINK? (15 minutes)

1. Ask students to read the questions and reflect on their answers.

2. Seat students in small groups and assign roles: a group leader to make sure everyone contributes, a note-taker to record the group's ideas, a reporter to share the group's ideas with the class, and a timekeeper to watch the clock.

3. Give students five minutes to discuss the questions. Call time if conversations are winding down. Allow them an extra minute or two if necessary.

4. Call on each group's reporter to share ideas with the class.

> **What Do You Think? Answers, pp. 154-155**
> Answers will vary but may include:
> 1. I've heard that people are beginning to turn used vegetable oil into gasoline.
> 2. I think I'm open-minded enough to try these new experiences. / No, I wouldn't do these things because I only trust remedies that I am familiar with.
> 3. I think that the hosts are neutral because they use reported speech to speak about what the guests and other experts have said. It's clear these ideas are not the host's.

Learning Outcome

Use the learning outcome to frame the purpose and relevance of Listening 1. Ask: *What did you learn from Listening 1 that prepares you to develop a marketing presentation?*

▶ *Listening and Speaking 5, page 155*

Listening Skill: Distinguishing between facts and opinions (20 minutes)

🔊 CD3, Track 5

1. Probe for previous knowledge by asking: *What is the difference between a fact and an opinion?*

2. Ask for volunteers to read the text aloud. Pause to provide additional explanation as needed.

3. Play the audio at the highlighted time.

4. Check comprehension by asking: *Why is distinguishing between facts and opinions important? What words identify facts? Opinions?*

▶ *Listening and Speaking 5, page 156*

A (10 minutes)
🔊 CD3, Track 6

1. Ask a student to read the instructions aloud.

2. Play the audio and have students complete the activity individually.

3. Direct students to share their ideas with a partner.

4. Check answers as a class.

> **Listening Skill A Answers, p. 156**
> 1. O, I think, unreliable;   2. F, can find online;
> 3. F, was developed, cost;   4. O, believes, could;
> 5. O, should;   6. F, reports;
> 7. F, is based on;   8. O, so expensive, probably;
> 9. O, best;   10. F, is sometimes used

B (10 minutes)
🔊 CD3, Track 7

1. Ask a volunteer to read the instructions. Check comprehension by asking: *What do you need to do during this activity?*

2. Play the audio and direct students to complete the sentences.

3. Have students review their answers with a partner.

4. Have pairs discuss with another pair whether the ad uses mostly facts or opinions, and if they would buy the product.

Listening Skill B Answers, pp. 156-157

1. amazing;   **2.** absolute best;
3. should be;   **4.** Thousands;
5. for two years; **6.** the most effective;
7. I believe;   **8.** probably

For additional practice with distinguishing between facts and opinions, have students visit *Q Online Practice*.

► *Listening and Speaking 5, page 157*

LISTENING 2: Boulder Bike-to-School Program Goes International

VOCABULARY (15 minutes)

1. Place students into groups of three to read the sentences, match the definitions, and identify a situation where the word might be used.

2. Check answers as a class.

> **MULTILEVEL OPTION**
>
> Pair lower-level students with higher-level students to choose several words to create short dialogs with, based on the situations they created for where the word might be used.

Vocabulary Answers, pp. 157-158
a. bar code; **b.** infrastructure; **c.** submit; **d.** propel;
e. substantial; **f.** outrageous; **g.** implement;
h. consistently; **i.** grant; **j.** incentive;
k. impromptu; **l.** buzzword

For additional practice with the vocabulary, have students visit *Q Online Practice*.

► *Listening and Speaking 5, page 159*

PREVIEW LISTENING 2 (5 minutes)

1. Direct students' attention to the photos and ask: *In the picture, kids are riding bikes. What are some positive effects of kids riding bikes to school?*

2. Preview the instructions and direct students to check off their ideas.

3. Have students discuss their answers in pairs.

4. Tell students they should review their selections after the Listening.

Preview Listening 2, p. 159
Answers will vary.

Listening 2 Background Note

Many organizations and governments offer programs to encourage commuters to bike. A report put out in the United States by Rails-to-Trails Conservancy (RTC) notes that, in the United States, 25 percent of journeys made are within a mile, an easy bike ride, and 50 percent are within three miles. According to RTC, by switching 9 percent of a city's population to biking, or walking, cities can see a reduction of 23 billion miles driven—thus reducing wear and tear on city roadways—and could save as much as $4.1 billion.

Teaching Note

Students may find the following words or phrases difficult.

catch on: (phr. v.) to become popular or fashionable

lofty: (adj.) deserving of praise because of its high moral quality (lofty ambitions, lofty praise)

trinket: (n.) a piece of jewelry or small decorative object that is not worth much money

sophisticated: (adj.) clever or complicated in the way that something works

LISTEN FOR MAIN IDEAS (5 minutes)

 CD3, Track 8

1. Have students preview the instructions and questions in pairs.

2. Play the audio and have students complete the activity individually.

3. Direct students to check answers with a partner. When done, elicit any questions students may have.

Listen for Main Ideas Answers, p. 159
1. "Freiker" combines *frequent* and *biker*. The program has to change its name because walkers are now included.
2. The program started out using punch cards, then bar codes, then RFID tags; now children ride past a "freikometer" and it registers their ride, so instead of monitoring, parents can help in the classroom.
3. The program encourages kids to use active transportation, which means they get themselves to school and don't get rides from their parents; riding bikes is a healthy activity and / helps develop Freiker "safe routes to school."

70   Unit 7

LISTEN FOR DETAILS (10 minutes)

 CD3, Track 9

A (10 minutes)

1. Direct students to read the statements before they listen again.

2. As you play the audio, have students listen and complete the sentences.

3. Have students compare answers with a partner.

4. Replay the audio so that partners can check their answers.

5. Go over the answers with the class.

> **Listen for Details A Answers, p. 160**
> 1. 50
> 2. Canada
> 3. iPod
> 4. Safe Routes to School, local bike shops, community groups

B (10 minutes)

1. Direct students to choose an answer on their own and then discuss with a partner.

2. Choose a few students to share answers aloud.

> **Listen for Details B Answers, p. 160**
> Explanations will vary.

For additional practice with listening comprehension, have students visit *Q Online Practice*.

WHAT DO YOU THINK?

A (10 minutes)

1. Ask students to read the questions and reflect on their answers.

2. Seat students in small groups and assign roles: a group leader to make sure everyone contributes, a note-taker to record the group's ideas, a reporter to share the group's ideas with the class, and a timekeeper to watch the clock.

3. Give students five minutes to discuss the questions. Call time if conversations are winding down. Allow them an extra minute or two if necessary.

4. Call on each group's reporter to share ideas with the class.

Activity A Answers, p. 160
Answers will vary but may include:
1. An advantage would be that children would likely continue making healthy choices. A disadvantage could be that children might only participate for the reward and not incorporate healthy living without it. Another way to achieve the goal is to have students come up with ideas for using active transportation. That way, they'll be interested in participating.
2. Such a program would only be in communities where people and businesses can afford the incentives offered in the program and where biking is safe.

B (5 minutes)

1. Have students continue working in their small groups to discuss the questions in Activity B. Tell them to choose a new leader, note-taker, reporter, and timekeeper.

2. Call on the new reporter to share the group's answers to the questions.

Learning Outcome

Use the learning outcome to frame the purpose and relevance of Listenings 1 and 2. Ask: *What did you learn from Listenings 1 and 2 that prepares you to develop a marketing presentation?*

Vocabulary Skill: Idioms and informal expressions (15 minutes)

1. Probe students' previous knowledge by asking: *How does your language change when you are trying to speak informally? Formally?*

2. Present the information on the Vocabulary Skill, stopping to elicit questions from the class.

3. Check comprehension: *What are some key reasons people use informal language? How can dictionaries help you know when you've found an informal word?*

Skill Note

When teaching formal and informal language, remind students of situations in which speaking respectfully is required, such as when addressing teachers or meeting new people. Point out that just because other students are peers doesn't mean they prefer to be spoken to informally. Emphasize that, if in doubt, it's often best to speak to a person formally at first.

1. Place students into pairs and give each pair a learner's dictionary.

2. Direct students to look through the dictionary and find seven examples of informal speech.

3. Direct students to create a dialog about where ideas come from using the new examples of informal language that they've found.

4. Have pairs present their dialogs to the class.

▶ *Listening and Speaking 5, page 162*

A (10 minutes)

1. Place students into pairs and preview the instructions.

2. Provide each pair with a dictionary and direct them to complete the activity.

3. Go over the answers with the class.

> **Activity A Answers, p. 162**
> **1.** news, rumors;
> **2.** will happen very soon;
> **3.** here is the situation…;
> **4.** to gain popularity, to understand;
> **5.** to implement something;
> **6.** superior to, of better quality than;
> **7.** to conclude, to complete, to finish;
> **8.** thrilled with, delighted with, very enthusiastic

B (10 minutes)
🔊 CD3, Track 10

1. Read the instructions and have a volunteer summarize them to ensure understanding.

2. Ask students to complete the activity individually. Play the audio.

3. Have students check their answers in pairs and use a dictionary if needed. Review answers as a class.

> **Activity B Answers, pp. 162-163**
> **1.** a big deal;
> Meaning: something that is important or exciting
> **2.** buzzed with;
> Meaning: to be full of excitement, activity, and so on
> **3.** kind of flaky;
> Meaning: odd or eccentric; a bit crazy
> **4.** light bulb went off;
> Meaning: to get a good idea

5. (take her idea and) run with it
   Meaning: to accept or start to use a new idea
6. shoot for the moon;
   Meaning: try to achieve or attain a goal that seems out of reach; to take a great risk in order to gain a great reward

Tip for Success (1 minute)

Read the tip aloud and use the Internet to demonstrate this tip, if possible.

 For additional practice with informal vs. formal language, have students visit *Q Online Practice*.

▶ *Listening and Speaking 5, page 164*

SPEAKING

Grammar: Noun clauses (20 minutes)

1. Probe for previous knowledge by asking: *What is a noun clause? Can you provide an example?*

2. Ask for volunteers to read the text aloud. Pause to provide additional explanation as needed.

3. Check comprehension by asking: *What are noun clauses? Why are noun clauses used?*

4. Ask volunteers to provide example sentences using noun clauses according to the provided guidelines.

Skill Note

Review the purposes of the noun clauses presented in this skill. Noun clauses with *if/whether* can be used to express uncertainty (e.g., *She wonders whether the school will be open tomorrow*). Noun clauses with *wh*-question words can be used to add more information to a verb (e.g., *He wants to know what he is going to do tomorrow.*)

▶ *Listening and Speaking 5, page 165*

A (10 minutes)

1. Have a student read the instructions for the activity. Do the first item as a class to model the activity.

2. Have students complete the activity individually and compare their answers with a partner.

3. Go over the answers with the class.

Activity A Answers, p. 165

1. She believes <u>the container clinics, ultimately, could make portable medicine a reality for people in countries that need it most.</u>
2. I've had patients in the last twenty years who told me <u>that relatives of theirs, older relatives working in the garden, had accidently got stung on their hands by a bee,</u> and their arthritis got better.
3. And I might also add <u>that we also include walkers now, um, as part of the program.</u>
4. We see no reason <u>why, if retrofitting is done on a mass scale, these containers couldn't come in for well under $1,500 apiece.</u>
5. Some compounds in bee venom might affect <u>how the body transmits pain signals to the brain,</u> but it's hard to know for sure.
6. He told <u>me how this grew from a handful of kids at Crestview Elementary School in Boulder into an international program.</u>

MULTILEVEL OPTION

Have lower-level students complete the activity in pairs. Have higher-level students do the same, but direct them to also write a different noun clause to replace the given noun clause in each sentence.

Tip for Success (1 minute)

1. Ask a volunteer to read the tip aloud.
2. Ask the class if they have noticed the omission of that in speech.

B (10 minutes)

1. Preview the instructions and place students into pairs. Model the activity by reading through the example as a class.
2. Direct students to complete the activity with a partner. Offer support as needed.
3. Review answers as a class.

Activity B Answers, p. 165

1. He told his boss that his coworker had stolen his idea.
2. We aren't sure if we want to sell it online.
3. I need to find out where they developed the prototype.
4. It's not clear how they raised enough money to give away iPods.
5. I don't understand why we can't convince people to get stung by bees.
6. They are trying to decide if they can convince the public to buy it.

7. We are trying to find out when the product was featured on the air.
8. The group was worried that the incentive could be seen as too outrageous.

 For additional practice with noun clauses, have students visit *Q Online Practice*.

▶ *Listening and Speaking 5, page 166*

Pronunciation: Conditional modals: affirmative and negative (15 minutes)

 CD3, Track 11

1. Present the information on reduced forms, playing the audio at the highlighted time.
2. Check comprehension. Ask: *What is an example of a reduced form? How can you tell the difference between affirmative and negative forms?*

A (10 minutes)
 CD3, Track 12

1. Direct students to preview the instructions.
2. Play the audio, and have student complete the activity individually.
3. Put students in pairs to discuss their answers.
4. Check answers as a class and practice pronunciation of forms.

Activity A Answers, p. 166

1. negative;   2. affirmative;   3. affirmative;
4. negative;   5. negative;   6. negative;
7. affirmative;   8. negative

B (10 minutes)
 CD3, Track 13

1. Ask for a volunteer to read the instructions.
2. Have students practice in pairs. Remind them to use reduced sounds when speaking.
3. Play the audio for students to check their own pronunciation. Direct students to practice again.

 For additional practice with conditional modals: affirmative and negative, have students visit *Q Online Practice*.

▶ *Listening and Speaking 5, page 167*

Speaking Skill: Using formal and informal language (10 minutes)

1. Ask: *In what situations do you use formal language? Informal language?*

2. Present the information on this skill to the class.

3. Check comprehension: *What is register? What are some features of each type of register?*

▶ *Listening and Speaking 5, page 168*

A (10 minutes)

1. Have a volunteer read the instructions for the activity aloud, and preview the situations as a class.

2. Place students into pairs to complete the activity.

3. Discuss answers as a class.

B (15 minutes)

1. Working in the same pairs, have students compose a conversation using appropriate register.

2. Have students practice their conversations.

3. Direct students to present their conversations to other pairs.

 For additional practice with using formal and informal language, have students visit *Q Online Practice*.

21ST CENTURY SKILLS

Increasing worldwide access to technology and travel bring people into contact in multiple contexts, requiring speakers to adapt their language appropriately. One hour, a person might be in a meeting with colleagues and, in the next. at a company social mixer. Practicing formal and informal registers will prove valuable as students enter an increasingly interconnected workplace. On pieces of paper, write situations such as "in the elevator with coworkers," "at a social lunch," etc., and have pairs select a situation to role-play and then perform for the class. After each role-play, discuss the register and language used.

Unit Assignment: Market a new idea

Unit Question (5 minutes)

Refer students back to the ideas they discussed at the beginning of the unit about how people come up with new ideas. Cue students if necessary by asking specific questions about the content of the unit: *What new ideas did we learn about? How were they formed?*

Learning Outcome

1. Tie the Unit Assignment to the unit learning outcome. Say: *The outcome for this unit is to develop a marketing presentation. This Unit Assignment is going to let you show your skill by giving a presentation.*

2. Explain that you are going to use a rubric similar to their self-assessment rubric on p. 170 to grade their Unit Assignment. You can also share a copy of the Unit Assignment Rubric (on p. 76 of this *Teacher's Handbook*) with students.

Consider the Ideas (5 minutes)

CD3, Track 14

A (5 minutes)

1. Preview the instructions for the activity.

2. Remind students to pay special attention to the language used in each advertisement.

3. Play the audio and have students take notes.

4. Place students into pairs to compare notes.

▶ *Listening and Speaking 5, page 169*

B (10 minutes)

Place students into groups of four to discuss the questions. Circulate around the room to offer support as needed.

> **Consider the Ideas B Answers, p. 165**
> Answers will vary.

Critical Q: Expansion Activity

Invent (10 minutes)

1. Read the Critical Thinking Tip from page 169.

2. Bring in several pictures that represent problems (e.g., a photo of extreme weather, a broken-down car, etc.).

3. Hold each picture up in turn and ask: *What do you think the problem is in this picture?* After students identify the problem, ask them to identify some possible solutions. Remind students that, at the early stages of invention, it's important to create as many solutions as possible. Emphasize that now is the time for brainstorming—evaluating actual ideas comes later.

Prepare and Speak

Gather Ideas

A (10–15 minutes)

1. Have students work with a partner to complete the activity.

2. Preview the chart and tell students: *Unlike some of the photos we just looked at, sometimes the problems that we need to solve are small.* Discuss possible solutions or inventions for the problems.

3. Direct students to fill in the chart. Circulate around the room to provide support and modeling.

4. Once their charts are completed, have pairs compare their answers.

Organize Ideas

B (10 minutes)

1. Preview the instructions to the activity and the steps students will need to follow. Ask a student to summarize the steps.

2. Have students work with their same partner.

3. Direct students to write outlines and note cards.

▶ *Listening and Speaking 5, page 170*

Speak

C (20 minutes)

1. Give pairs ample time to practice their presentations at least twice.

2. Call on pairs to present to the class.

3. Use the Unit Assignment Rubric on p. 76 of this *Teacher's Handbook* to score each student's presentation.

4. Alternatively, divide the class into large groups and have students give their presentations to their group. Have listeners complete the Unit Assignment Rubric.

Alternative Unit Assignments

Assign or have students choose one of these assignments to do instead of, or in addition to, the Unit Assignment.

1. Here are two innovative ideas that use old ideas in new ways: (1) A clock invented by MIT students jumps off the table and hides so you have to get out of bed to turn it off;

(2) An air bag designed by a Japanese inventor can be worn by the elderly to prevent injuries when falling. Discuss your reactions to these ideas. Do you think these are marketable ideas? What would be the most effective ways to sell these products, and to whom?

2. What alternative therapies are people going back to these days that are based on traditional medicine?

3. Present some innovative ideas you have thought about or heard about, even though they might be unrealistic to actually make.

 For an additional unit assignment, have students visit *Q Online Practice*.

Check and Reflect

Check

A (10 minutes)

1. Direct students to read and complete the self-assessment rubric.

2. Ask for a show of hands for how many students gave all or mostly *yes* answers.

3. Congratulate them on their success. Remind students that they can refer to the rubric before they begin the Unit Assignment so they can focus on the skills needed to do well. Have them discuss with a partner what they can improve.

Reflect

B (5–10 minutes)

Ask students to consider the questions in pairs or groups of three. When the conversations have tapered off, ask: *What was difficult about "selling" a new idea? Why? What skills did you practice when completing this Unit Assignment that you can use in other areas of your life—in school or at work? Why?*

▶ *Listening and Speaking 5, page 171*

Track Your Success (5 minutes)

1. Have students circle the words they have learned in this unit. Suggest that students go back through the unit to review any words they have forgotten.

2. Have students check the skills they have mastered. If students need more practice to feel confident about their proficiency in a skill, point out the page numbers and encourage them to review.

3. Read the Learning Outcome aloud. Ask students if they feel that they have met the outcome.

Unit Assignment Rubric

Student name: _____

Date: _____

20 points = Presentation element was completely successful (at least 90% of the time).
15 points = Presentation element was mostly successful (at least 70% of the time).
10 points = Presentation element was partially successful (at least 50% of the time).
 0 points = Presentation element was not successful.

Market a New Idea	20 points	15 points	10 points	0 points
Student spoke fluently and used informal and formal language appropriately.				
Student used noun clauses correctly.				
Student used at least five vocabulary items from the unit.				
Student pronounced affirmative and negative conditional modals correctly.				
Student used facts and opinions appropriately as he or she spoke.				

Total points: _____

Comments:

8

Unit QUESTION

How do people react to change?

Change

LISTENING • recognizing attitudes
VOCABULARY • phrasal verbs
GRAMMAR • gerunds and infinitives
PRONUNCIATION • consonant variations
SPEAKING • paraphrasing

LEARNING OUTCOME

Interview a classmate and report on that person's attitude concerning change.

▶ *Listening and Speaking 5, page 173*

Preview the Unit

Learning Outcome

1. Ask for a volunteer to read the unit skills, then the unit learning outcome.

2. Explain: *This is what you are expected to be able to do by the unit's end. The learning outcome explains how you are going to be evaluated. With this outcome in mind, you should focus on learning these skills (Listening, Vocabulary, Grammar, Pronunciation, Speaking) that will support your goal of "interviewing a classmate about change." This can also help you act as mentors in the classroom to help the other students meet this outcome.*

A (10 minutes)

1. Ask the class: *Do you like when things change? Why or why not?*

2. Put students in pairs or small groups to discuss the first two questions.

3. Call on volunteers to share their ideas with the class. Ask questions: *What do you think the most common reaction to change is?*

4. Focus students' attention on the photo. Have a volunteer describe the photo to the class. Read the question aloud. Ask: *How does this photo represent change in our world?*

Activity A Answers, p. 173
Possible answers:
1. My family has moved four times because my father is a salesman who has worked out of different offices.
2. Living with my aunt for a while, moving across the country; I prefer to know what to expect in my life.

3. She is reacting to change because she is using new technology to communicate while performing a task that has been done the same way for centuries.

B (10 minutes)

1. Introduce the Unit Question, "How do people react to change?" Ask related questions to help students prepare for answering the more abstract Unit Question: *Do you think people you know like change? Why or why not?*

2. Label four pieces of poster paper: *Avoid Change, Seek Change, Scared of Change*, and *Ambivalent Toward Change* and place them in the corners of the room.

3. Ask students to consider the Unit Question and then to stand in the corner next to the poster that best represents their answer to the question.

4. Direct the groups in each corner to discuss the reasons for their answer. Tell them to choose a secretary to record the answers on the posters.

5. Call on volunteers from each corner to share their opinions with the class.

6. Leave the posters up for students to refer back to at the end of the unit.

Activity B Answers, p. 173
Possible answers: I think that people can be afraid of change because they are unsure of how their new situation will work out. / I believe that a lot of people embrace change because there's always something good in something new.

The Q Classroom (5 minutes)

🔊 CD3, Track 15

1. Play The Q Classroom. Use the example from the audio to help students continue the conversation. Ask: *How did the students answer the question? Do you agree or disagree with their ideas? Why?*

LISTEN FOR MAIN IDEAS (10 minutes)

🔊 CD3, Track 16

1. Preview the instructions and the questions as a class.

2. Play the audio and have students complete the activity individually.

3. Place students into pairs and have them read their statements. Check as a class.

> **Listen for Main Ideas Answers, p. 177**
> Answers will vary but may include:
> **1.** The herders feel caught between the world of the urban Mongolian elite and the world of their nomadic tribe.
> **2.** They are struggling to keep up the traditional nomadic way of life herding the reindeer.
> **3.** Sanjeem is worried that if they settle, the herders will lose their way of life and identity as a people.

LISTEN FOR DETAILS (10 minutes)

🔊 CD3, Track 17

A (10 minutes)

1. Direct students to preview the statements in Activity B before they listen again.

2. As you play the audio, have students listen and take notes in the T-chart.

3. Have students compare answers with a partner.

4. Replay the audio so that partners can check their answers.

5. Go over the answers with the class.

> **Listen for Details A Answers, p. 177**
> T-chart: Answers will vary.

B (10 minutes)

1. Preview the instructions. Complete the first statement as a class.

2. Direct students to complete the activity.

3. Have students compare answers with a partner. Then call on volunteers to read statements aloud.

> **Listen for Details B Answers, pp. 177-178**
> **1.** grass; **2.** 207; **3.** milk, cheese, yogurt;
> **4.** veterinary care and financial help;
> **5.** veterinary; **6.** disease, wolves; **7.** "hope"

 For additional practice with listening comprehension, have students visit *Q Online Practice*.

EXPANSION ACTIVITY: Giving the News (20 minutes)

🔊 CD3, Track 16

1. Replay the audio from Listening 1, asking students to take notes so that they can summarize the story. Use the Listen for Details activity to aid in this reconstruction.

2. Pair students to create a presentation where they will retell the news story, using five of the new vocabulary words they've learned.

3. Have groups present their "newscast" to the class.

Q WHAT DO YOU THINK? (10 minutes)

1. Ask students to read the questions and reflect on their answers.

2. Seat students in small groups and assign roles: a group leader to make sure everyone contributes, a note-taker to record the group's ideas, a reporter to share the group's ideas with the class, and a timekeeper to watch the clock.

3. Give students five minutes to discuss the questions. Call time if conversations are winding down. Allow them an extra minute or two if necessary.

4. Call on each group's reporter to share ideas with the class.

> **MULTILEVEL OPTION**
>
> Pair higher-level students with lower-level students. Have the higher-level student interview the lower-level student using the questions from "What Do You Think?" and record their answers to retell to the class.

> **What Do You Think? Answers, p. 178**
> Possible answers:
> **1.** Elders resist change because many times they know no other way of life, and younger people embrace change because new things can seem exciting.
> **2.** Some people might want the nomads to settle so that it'll be easier to keep track of them.
> **3.** These nomads have been living this way for a long time, and I believe that their lifestyle can withstand change.

Learning Outcome

Use the learning outcome to frame the purpose and relevance of Listening 1. Ask: *What did you learn from Listening 1 that prepares you to interview a classmate about change?*

▶ *Listening and Speaking 5, page 179*

Listening Skill: Recognizing attitudes

(10 minutes)

🔊 CD3, Track 18

1. Present the information in the Listening Skill box. Play the highlighted audio at the appropriate time.

2. Check comprehension by asking questions: *What are some common intonation patterns, and what does each convey?*

▶ *Listening and Speaking 5, page 180*
🔊 CD3, Track 19

A (10 minutes)

1. Ask a volunteer to read the instructions.

2. Play the audio and direct students to check the attitudes that they infer from the audio.

3. Pair students to compare answers, then check answers as a class.

> **Listening Skill A Answers, p. 180**
> 1. Disagreement   2. Sadness
> 3. Disagreement   4. Disbelief or Surprise
> 5. Excitement or Interest   6. Sadness
> 7. Disbelief or Surprise   8. Excitement or Interest

B (10 minutes)

🔊 CD3, Track 20

1. Preview the instructions and the choices as a class.

2. Play the audio and have students select their answers.

3. Place students into pairs to compare answers and discuss how they made their choices.

> **Listening Skill B Answers, p.180**
> Explanations will vary.
> 1. a; the speaker uses fairly neutral intonation with some varied pitch indicating interest; she stresses the words "we choose," "one way," and "even," and the stress helps to convey some excitement/enthusiasm for the subject; she also uses phrases like "still possible," which indicate optimism.
> 2. b; The speaker uses a lot of high rising intonation signaling disbelief, on phrases like "way, way past." He uses rising intonation on "they basically didn't have homes anymore," but he is not directly critical of them or disagreeing with their lifestyle. Arguably, he also expresses enthusiasm/interest for the topic by using varied pitch.

 For additional practice with recognizing attitudes, have students visit *Q Online Practice*.

▶ *Listening and Speaking 5, page 181*

LISTENING 2: High-Tech Nomads

VOCABULARY (15 minutes)

1. Place students into pairs to read the definitions and complete the sentences with the correct words.

2. Check answers as a class, and then have pairs create one new sentence for each vocabulary item.

3. Direct a few volunteers to read their sentences. Correct as necessary.

> **Vocabulary Answers, pp. 181-182**
> 1. marginal
> 2. roots
> 3. intrepid
> 4. psyche
> 5. breakthroughs
> 6. stability
> 7. irony
> 8. accomplish
> 9. payoff
> 10. mundane
> 11. evolved
> 12. attention span

 For additional practice with the vocabulary, have students visit *Q Online Practice*.

▶ *Listening and Speaking 5, page 182*

PREVIEW LISTENING 2 (5 minutes)

1. Direct students' attention to the photos and ask: *How might the life of the man in this photo be described as nomadic?*

2. Ask students to check the descriptions they think apply to a high-tech nomad. Tell students to review their answers after the Listening.

Listening 2 Background Note

Many people who travel a lot have frequent-flyer status. A frequent-flyer program is an incentive program where the more miles a person flies with one carrier, the more perks the person receives. Some programs allow flyers to upgrade their seats for free, get free flights, and rent cars for free—all if they earn a certain number of miles. Travelers all over the world take part in these types of programs, and those who fly all the time, like the high-tech nomads we will hear about, reap huge benefits.

Teaching Note

Students may find the following words or phrases difficult.

cranky: (adj.) bad-tempered; in a bad mood

savannah: (n.) a wide, flat, open area of land that is covered with grass but has few trees

drive somebody nuts: to make somebody very angry, crazy, etc., or to make them do something extreme

pundit: (n.) a person who knows a lot about a subject and often talks about it in public; an expert

in abeyance: (phr.) not being used, or being stopped for a period of time

venture capitalist: (phr.) someone who invests money in a new company to help it develop

▶ *Listening and Speaking 5, page 183*

LISTEN FOR MAIN IDEAS (10 minutes)

◉ CD3, Track 21

1. Preview the instructions and each of the questions.

2. Play the audio and have students complete the activity in pairs.

3. Discuss answers as a class.

Listen for Main Ideas Answers, p. 183
1. Garreau believes that high-tech nomads are successful, nomadic, crazy, plugged-in, rich, and hard-working.
2. They choose this life because they need to stay connected to the changing world and enjoy the stimulation.
3. They give up stability such as a permanent home, a community, and a certain amount of peace.
4. Garreau would say that despite their technology, in the end they need face-to-face contact to get the job done.

LISTEN FOR DETAILS (10 minutes)

◉ CD3, Track 22

1. Direct students to preview the details before they listen again.

2. As you play the audio, have students listen and check the details that they hear.

3. Have students compare answers with a partner.

4. Replay the audio so that partners can check their answers.

5. Go over the answers with the class.

Listen for Details Answers, pp. 183-184
Correct details: Check (✓) items 1, 2, 7, 8, and 9.

 For additional practice with listening comprehension, have students visit *Q Online Practice*.

▶ *Listening and Speaking 5, page 184*

Q WHAT DO YOU THINK?

A (10 minutes)

1. Ask students to read the questions and reflect on their answers.

2. Seat students in small groups and assign roles: a group leader to make sure everyone contributes, a note-taker to record the group's ideas, a reporter to share the group's ideas with the class, and a timekeeper to watch the clock.

3. Give students five minutes to discuss the questions. Call time if conversations are winding down. Allow them an extra minute or two if necessary.

4. Call on each group's reporter to share ideas with the class.

Activity A Answers, p. 184
Possible answers:
1. The speakers seem to be in awe of these high-tech nomads, but I think their lives sound tiring and lonely.
2. I do okay meeting new people and being in new places, but I don't want to travel as much as high-tech nomads do.
3. I check social networking sites to stay connected to my friends; technology has allowed me to stay in touch better.

B (5 minutes)

1. Have students continue working in their small groups to discuss the questions in Activity B. Tell them to choose a new leader, recorder, reporter, and timekeeper.

2. Call on the new reporter to share the group's answers to the questions.

Learning Outcome

Use the learning outcome to frame the purpose and relevance of Listenings 1 and 2. Ask: *What did you learn from Listenings 1 and 2 that prepares you to interview a classmate about change?*

▶ *Listening and Speaking 5, page 185*

Vocabulary Skill: Phrasal verbs (10 minutes)

1. Present the information on phrasal verbs.

2. Check comprehension: *What are some examples of phrasal verbs? What others do you know? What can you say about the formality of phrasal verbs?*

Skill Note

Tell students that sometimes the meanings of phrasal verbs are not predictable from their component words. Write the following list of phrasal verbs and their definitions on the board: *give back* (to return), *run away* (to leave quickly), *fall through* (to not happen), and *drop off* (to deliver something). Discuss each phrasal verb and give example sentences to demonstrate their meaning.

▶ *Listening and Speaking 5, page 186*

A (10 minutes)

1. Direct students to complete the activity individually. Ensure students have dictionaries.

2. Ask students to compare their answers in pairs.

3. Go over the answers with the class.

> **Activity A Answers, p. 186**
> **1.** away, S; **2.** up, S; **3.** back, S; **4.** at, I;
> **5.** away, S; **6.** up with, I; **7.** out, S; **8.** up, S;
> **9.** up on, I; **10.** back, I; **11.** down, S; **12.** in, I

▶ *Listening and Speaking 5, page 187*

B (10 minutes)

1. Preview the instructions and place students into pairs.

2. Model the activity by reviewing the example.

3. Direct students to complete the task and check answers as a class.

> **Activity B Answers, p. 187**
> **1.** stay away, x
> **2.** give up, I am trying to give it up.
> **3.** pick up, …They have no central place to pick it up.
> **4.** pick up on, X
> **5.** turn in, X
> **6.** give (that item) back/away, give it away/give it back.

 For additional practice with phrasal verbs, have students visit *Q Online Practice*.

▶ *Listening and Speaking 5, page 188*

SPEAKING

Grammar: Gerunds and infinitives
(20 minutes)

1. Probe for previous knowledge by asking students what they know about gerunds and infinitives.

2. Present the information to students by choosing volunteers to alternate reading the text with you.

3. Check comprehension by asking questions: *How are gerunds formed? How are infinitives formed? What are some rules for when to use them?*

Skill Note

Gerunds and infinitives can also be used as appositives; that is, they can be used to provide more information about a noun. For example, in the sentence, *"She gave him a suggestion to eat all of his vegetables,"* the infinitive tells what suggestion was given. And in the sentence *"His most recent proposal, building a new gymnasium, is too extravagant for our small budget,"* the gerund modifies the existing noun phrase. Appositives made with gerunds and infinitives tend to modify more abstract nouns, such as *proposal, suggestion, hope, desire, request,* etc.

▶ *Listening and Speaking 5, page 189*

A (10 minutes)

1. Direct students to preview the statements and complete the task with a partner.

2. Put students in groups of four to discuss and compare their answers.

3. Call on volunteers to share their ideas with the class. Correct as needed.

> **Activity A Answers, p. 189**
> **1.** maintaining OR to maintain;
> **2.** moving;
> **3.** to embrace;
> **4.** to cope;
> **5.** staying;
> **6.** using;
> **7.** to travel

B (10 minutes)

1. Place students into pairs and have them preview the instructions and questions. Answer any questions.

2. Direct the pairs to complete the activity.

Tip for Success (2 minutes)

1. Ask a volunteer to read the tip aloud.

2. Ask students to look up *deny* in their dictionaries to see where this information is located.

 For additional practice with gerunds and infinitives, have students visit *Q Online Practice*.

Pronunciation: Consonant variations
(15 minutes)

🔊 CD3, Track 23

1. Present the information to students, playing the audio at the highlighted point.

2. Check comprehension by asking questions: *What is a final consonant? What consonants can change their sounds?*

3. Have pairs practice reading the examples.

▶ *Listening and Speaking 5, page 191*

A (10 minutes)

🔊 CD3, Track 24

1. Preview the instructions and the examples.

2. Direct students to complete the activity individually as they listen to the audio.

3. Play the audio.

4. Choose volunteers to produce the sounds and correct pronunciation as necessary.

B (10 minutes)

🔊 CD3, Track 25

1. Direct students to choose the words which feature the sound by saying each word with a partner.

2. Play the audio and have students make corrections to their answers as needed.

3. Check answers as a class.

> **Activity B Answers, p. 191**
> **1.** b, c, d; **2.** a, b, c; **3.** a, c, d; **4.** a, b, d;
> **5.** a, b, c; **6.** a, b, d; **7.** a, c, d

▶ *Listening and Speaking 5, page 192*

C (10 minutes)

🔊 CD3, Track 26

1. Play the audio and have students circle the words with the highlighted features.

2. Check answers as a class.

> **Activity C Answers, p. 192**
> Welcome **to** the world of the high-**tech** nomad. **Writer** Joel Garreau **investigated** this unique breed of traveler for *The Washington Post*. And he sat down with us recently **to tell** us what he learned.

 For additional practice with consonant variations, have students visit *Q Online Practice*.

Speaking Skill: Paraphrasing (10 minutes)

🔊 CD3, Track 27

1. Present the information on paraphrasing to the class, playing the audio at the indicated time.

2. Check comprehension: *Why is paraphrasing useful? What are some tips for paraphrasing?*

21ST CENTURY SKILLS

Skilled conversationalists often paraphrase what they hear a speaker saying. While listeners don't want to paraphrase everything a person says, repeating back what a speaker has said will help the listener understand the speaker's message. It also shows the speaker that he or she is actively being listened to. Place students into groups and have them brainstorm situations where paraphrasing would be useful (e.g., after listening to directions). Discuss answers as a class.

▶ *Listening and Speaking 5, page 193*

A (10 minutes)

1. Pair students. Read the instructions and discuss the example as a class.

2. Direct students to begin the activity. Have partners take turns paraphrasing. Offer support as needed.

3. Ask volunteers to share a paraphrase with the class.

> **Activity A Answers, p. 193**
> Answers will vary.

Tip for Success (2 minutes)

1. Read the tip aloud.
2. Ask: *Why do you think it is important to give credit to the source of an idea?*

B (10 minutes)

1. Preview the instructions and model the activity by reading through the example.
2. Place students into pairs and direct them to complete the task. Offer support as needed.
3. Choose a few pairs to present their role-plays to the rest of the class.

   Activity B Answers, p. 194
   Answers will vary.

   For additional practice with paraphrasing, have students visit *Q Online Practice*.

Unit Assignment:
Conduct a personal interview

Unit Question (5 minutes)

Refer students back to the ideas they discussed at the beginning of the unit about how people react to change. Cue students if necessary by asking specific questions about the content of the unit: *How did people in Listening 1 and 2 react to change? Why?*

Learning Outcome

1. Tie the Unit Assignment to the unit learning outcome. Say: *The outcome for this unit is to interview a classmate and report on that person's attitudes concerning change. This Unit Assignment is going to let you conduct an interview and report on your findings.*
2. Explain that you are going to use a rubric similar to their self-assessment rubric on p. 196 to grade their Unit Assignment. You can also share a copy of the Unit Assignment Rubric (on p. 86 of this *Teacher's Handbook*) with students.

Consider the Ideas (10 minutes)

1. Preview the instructions and ask students to work in groups of four.

2. Direct the groups to read through the quotes, paraphrase the ideas, and answer the questions.
3. As a class, review some of the groups' paraphrases.

Prepare and Speak

Gather Ideas

A (15 minutes)

1. Place students into new pairs.
2. Preview the activity and direct pairs to discuss the quotations and list questions in their notebooks.

Critical Q: Expansion Activity

Defend (15 minutes)

1. Read the Critical Thinking Tip from page 195.
2. Ask students to individually create two quotes that explain values or beliefs that are central to their lives. Tell students that they'll present their quotes to their peers, and they'll have to explain (or defend) their ideas.
3. Place students into groups of five, and direct them to share their quotes. Direct group members to ask questions about the quotes so that the speaker will have to defend and explain his or her ideas.

Organize Ideas

Tip for Success (3 minutes)

1. Ask students to read the tip silently.
2. Ask students: *Do you find it difficult or easy to maintain eye contact? Why or why not?*

B (15 minutes)

1. Preview the instructions and direct partners to begin to interview each other using their questions from Activity A.
2. Next, ask students to ask each other which quote from Consider the Ideas best fits their attitude.

Speak

C (25 minutes)

1. Have students summarize their findings, and then direct them to give their presentations to the class.

2. Use the Unit Assignment Rubric on p. 86 of this *Teacher's Handbook* to score each student's presentation.

3. Alternatively, divide the class into large groups and have students give their presentations to their group. Have listeners complete the Unit Assignment Rubric.

Alternative Unit Assignments

Assign or have students choose one of these assignments to do instead of, or in addition to, the Unit Assignment.

1. Explain whether you would like to work for a temporary service where your job might change every few weeks or months, or whether you would prefer a more permanent, long-term job. Point out the advantages and disadvantages of each situation.

2. Discuss the ways your culture has changed from your grandparents' to your parents' to your generation.

3. Present some ideas on ways society can make it easier for cultures that are not part of the mainstream either to preserve their customs and traditions in a changing world or to embrace change and assimilate into the mainstream.

 For an additional unit assignment, have students visit *Q Online Practice*.

Check and Reflect

Check

A (10 minutes)

1. Direct students to read and complete the self-assessment rubric.

2. Ask for a show of hands for how many students gave all or mostly *yes* answers.

3. Congratulate them on their success. Remind students that they can refer to the rubric before they begin the Unit Assignment so they can focus on the skills needed to do well. Have them discuss with a partner what they can improve.

Reflect

B (5-10 minutes)

Ask students to consider the questions in pairs or groups of three. When the conversations have tapered off, ask: *What was a challenge of reporting on information you gathered in an interview? Why?*

▶ *Listening and Speaking 5, page 197*

Track Your Success (5 minutes)

1. Have students circle the words they have learned in this unit. Suggest that students go back through the unit to review any words they have forgotten.

2. Have students check the skills they have mastered. If students need more practice to feel confident about their proficiency in a skill, point out the page numbers and encourage them to review.

3. Read the Learning Outcome aloud. Ask students if they feel that they have met the outcome.

Unit Assignment Rubric

Student name: _____

Date: _____

20 points = Presentation element was completely successful (at least 90% of the time).
15 points = Presentation element was mostly successful (at least 70% of the time).
10 points = Presentation element was partially successful (at least 50% of the time).
 0 points = Presentation element was not successful.

Conduct a Personal Interview	20 points	15 points	10 points	0 points
Student spoke clearly and at a good speed about the topic.				
Student used phrasal verbs appropriately.				
Student used gerunds and infinitives correctly.				
Student pronounced consonant sounds correctly.				
Student paraphrased appropriately.				

Total points: _____

Comments:

UNIT 9

Unit QUESTION
Where should the world's energy come from?

Energy

LISTENING • listening for cause and effect	**LEARNING OUTCOME**
VOCABULARY • Greek and Latin word roots	
GRAMMAR • adverb clauses	Participate in a class debate in which you
PRONUNCIATION • sentence rhythm	support opinions concerning the future
SPEAKING • debating opinions	of energy.

▶ *Listening and Speaking 5, page 199*

Preview the Unit

Learning Outcome

1. Ask for a volunteer to read the unit skills, then the unit learning outcome.

2. Explain: *This is what you are expected to be able to do by the unit's end. The learning outcome explains how you are going to be evaluated. With this outcome in mind, you should focus on learning these skills (Listening, Vocabulary, Grammar, Pronunciation, Speaking) that will support your goal of "participating in a class debate." This can also help you act as mentors in the classroom to help the other students meet this outcome.*

A (15 minutes)

1. Ask the class: *What kind of energy do you use throughout the day?*

2. Put students in pairs or small groups to discuss the first two questions.

3. Call on volunteers to share their ideas with the class. Ask questions: *What are the differences between non-renewable and renewable energy sources? Can you give examples of each?*

4. Focus students' attention on the photo. Have a volunteer describe the photo to the class. Read the question aloud. Ask: *What do you know about the energy featured in this photo?*

Activity A Answers, p. 199
Possible answers:
1. Our energy comes from Russia because they have large supplies of oil and gas.
2. Environmentalists care that energy comes from renewable sources because it is good for the planet. Solar and wind power are promising renewable energy choices.

3. This photo shows a solar energy plant, and solar energy is a renewable source of energy.

B (10 minutes)

1. Introduce the Unit Question, "Where should the world's energy come from?" Ask related questions to help students prepare for answering the more abstract Unit Question: *Why do we need to worry about where energy comes from?*

2. Tell students: *Let's start off our discussion by listing possible sources for where our energy should come from.*

3. Seat students in small groups and direct them to pass around a paper as quickly as they can, with each group member adding one item to the list. Give them two minutes to list ideas.

4. Call time and ask a reporter from each group to read the list aloud.

5. Use items from the list as a springboard for discussion: *Let's talk about new energy sources. What were some of your ideas?*

Activity B Answers, p. 199
Possible answers:
We should start getting more energy from the sun because the sun is always there, and we have the technology to turn sunlight into electricity cleanly.

The Q Classroom (5 minutes)
CD4, Track 2

1. Play The Q Classroom. Use the example from the audio to help students continue the conversation. Ask: *How did the students answer the question? Do you agree or disagree with their ideas? Why?*

2. Say: *In the audio, Yuna says that we need fossil fuels because the world is set up for them. Do you agree? Is it possible to set it up for other fuels?*

▶ *Listening and Speaking 5, page 200*

C (10 minutes)

1. Ask students to look over the pictures and discuss the sources in groups of three.

2. Discuss answers as a class. Ask students to support their ideas with details from the pictures.

D (10 minutes)

1. Working in the same groups, direct students to complete the task. Provide support as needed.

2. When done, choose a few volunteers to share their ideas with the class.

▶ *Listening and Speaking 5, page 201*

LISTENING

LISTENING 1: Nuclear Energy: Is It the Solution?

VOCABULARY (15 minutes)

1. Ask students if they have seen any of these vocabulary items before. If so, ask: *Where have you seen the word? What do you think it means?*

2. Have students complete the activity with a partner.

3. Call on volunteers to read their answers. After each has been read, ask the class if they agree with the match. Elicit a correction from the class if needed.

MULTILEVEL OPTION

Pair lower- and higher-level students together, and have them create a short dialog using several of the vocabulary words. Direct the higher-level students to make corrections to the writing as needed. Choose a pair or two to present their dialogs to the class.

Vocabulary Answers, p. 201-202
1. b; **2.** a; **3.** b; **4.** c; **5.** a; **6.** a;
7. a; **8.** c; **9.** c; **10.** a; **11.** a; **12.** b

 For additional practice with the vocabulary, have students visit *Q Online Practice*.

▶ *Listening and Speaking 5, page 203*

PREVIEW LISTENING 1 (5 minutes)

1. Direct students to look at the photo. Ask: *What do you know about nuclear energy?* Discuss answers as a class.

2. Have a volunteer read the directions aloud, and direct students to make their choices individually.

3. Pair students and have them share their ideas. Tell students they should review their answers after the Listening.

Listening 1 Background Note

Chernobyl, currently located in Ukraine, is often brought up when weighing a decision about bringing a nuclear reactor to a community. But what happened there on April 26, 1986? A burst of electricity, surging during an equipment test, ran through the system, and when the personnel tried to go into an emergency shutdown, more electricity surged and caused several explosions to occur. The explosions damaged one of the nuclear reactors in the facility, and nuclear material was shot into the air. The nuclear waste traveled on the winds as far away as Sweden, but radiation poisoning mostly affected Ukraine, Belarus, and Russia.

LISTEN FOR MAIN IDEAS (10 minutes)

 CD4, Track 3

A (10 minutes)

1. Preview the instructions for the activity.

2. Play the audio and have students choose their answers individually.

3. Place students into groups of three and have them review their answers. Then discuss as a class.

4. Replay the audio to highlight answers, if needed.

> **Listen for Main Ideas A Answers, pp. 203-204**
> **1.** b; **2.** a; **3.** b; **4.** a; **5.** a; **6.** b

▶ *Listening and Speaking 5, page 204*

LISTEN FOR DETAILS

CD4, Track 4

A (10 minutes)

1. Preview the instructions for the activity. Review previous knowledge by asking: *What are the benefits of organizing information in a T-chart?*

2. As you play the audio, have students listen and fill in the chart.

3. Have students compare answers with a partner.

4. Replay the audio so that partners can check their answers.

5. Go over the answers with the class.

> **Listen for Details Answers, p. 204**
> Answers will vary but may include:
> **For Nuclear Energy:** need to reduce fossil fuels; fossil fuels imported from other countries; fossil fuels pollute environment/cause climate change; nuclear energy is cleaner, safer, and more reliable; safe – no one in North America has been injured or died; supplies 70% of emission-free electricity; solar and wind are intermittent; face danger of energy shortage
> **Against Nuclear Energy:** producing nuclear energy/ uranium mines is risky; nuclear energy waste is radioactive; has to be stored/guarded; takes thousands of years to break down; can have accidents; need to develop solar and wind – low-cost, safe, renewable; nuclear power plants expensive

▶ *Listening and Speaking 5, page 205*

B (10 minutes)

1. Place students into pairs and preview the instructions and the statements as a class.

2. Direct students to use their notes to answer the questions. Offer support as needed.

> **Listen for Details B Answers, p. 205**
> 1. We have to import from other countries; fossil fuels pollute the environment and contribute to climate change; nuclear energy is cleaner, safer, and more reliable.
> 2. Waste is highly radioactive; we can have accidents; nuclear plants are expensive to build.
> 3. *Carbon-Free, Nuclear-Free*
> 4. Not a single person in North America has been injured or killed.
> 5. 70%
> 6. Wind, solar, hydroelectric
> 7. 50%
> 8. Energy from renewable sources isn't constant.

 For additional practice with listening comprehension, have students visit *Q Online Practice*.

WHAT DO YOU THINK? (10 minutes)

1. Ask students to read the questions and reflect on their answers.

2. Seat students in small groups and assign roles: a group leader to make sure everyone contributes, a note-taker to record the group's ideas, a reporter to share the group's ideas with the class, and a timekeeper to watch the clock.

3. Give students five minutes to discuss the questions. Call time if conversations are winding down. Allow them an extra minute or two if necessary.

4. Call on each group's reporter to share ideas with the class.

MULTILEVEL OPTION

Have lower-level students use notes from the T-chart to help them answer the questions, and have higher-level students ask and answer follow-up questions.

What Do You Think? Answers, pp. 205-206
Possible answers:
1. I agree with the anti-nuclear speaker because I believe there are safer ways to get our energy for our communities.
2. I think that solar has the most potential to be efficient if it is harnessed correctly and is the least risky option because the sun doesn't propose a new hazard.
3. Our greatest concern should be climate change because our energy consumption might be fueling drastic changes in global weather patterns.

Learning Outcome

Use the learning outcome to frame the purpose and relevance of Listening 1. Ask: *What did you learn from Listening 1 that prepares you to participate in a class debate on the future of energy?*

▶ *Listening and Speaking 5, page 206*

Listening Skill: Listening for cause and effect (15 minutes)

1. Present the information on the Listening Skill. Have students repeat the example sentences as you read them. Have students raise two fingers when saying the cause and one finger when saying the effect.

2. Check comprehension by asking questions: *What are some signal phrases for cause? Effect?*

▶ *Listening and Speaking 5, page 207*

A (10 minutes)

1. Preview the chart with the class.
2. Place students into pairs to fill out the chart with information they remember from the Listening.
3. Discuss answers as a class.

> **Listening Skill A Answers, p. 207**
> Answers will vary but may include:
> **1.** Cause: Because we can't provide enough ourselves.
> **2.** Effect: Emissions pollute the environment and contribute to global warming.
> **3.** Cause: They are intermittent sources.

B (5-10 minutes)

🔊 CD4, Track 5

1. Preview the instructions.
2. Play the audio and direct students to write the causes and effects for each energy source.
3. After students compare answers with a partner, check answers as a class.

> **Listening Skill B Answers, p. 207**
> **1.** Cause: corn requires water and fertilizer; Effect: new energy crops are being developed
> **2.** a. Cause: everyone is worried about gas prices; Effect: Japan has a new fuel for cars; b. Cause: hydrogen can be separated from water; Effect: hydrogen from water can fuel cars
> **3.** a. Cause: a lot of garbage in San Francisco; Effect: research project on using garbage; b. Cause: food leftovers placed in tank; Effect: gas is produced; c. Cause: chemical reaction in gas tank; Effect: electricity to power 80 homes a day; d. Cause: findings from the project; Effect: decrease garbage in the city

 For additional practice with listening for cause and effect, have students visit *Q Online Practice*.

EXPANSION ACTIVITY: Envisioning New Energy (20 minutes)

1. Say to students: *Some of the ideas for new energy sources we've heard about came from brainstorming sessions. What energy sources are we still missing? What ideas do you have for getting energy? Be creative—think of brand new sources.*
2. Have pairs brainstorm new sources of energy (e.g., getting electricity from the friction of people walking on sidewalks). Ask students to be prepared to explain how their idea might generate electricity.

3. Allow students ample time to practice their presentations before giving them to the class or large groups.

21ST CENTURY SKILLS

Innovation is an essential ingredient of the modern workplace. Businesses, and other organizations, thrive on new ideas—and today's great idea was often yesterday's unconventional afterthought. Encourage students to participate in mini-brainstorming sessions when confronted with challenges in their daily lives. Invite groups to brainstorm ideas for smart phone apps that would make their lives easier, and then share their ideas with the class.

▶ *Listening and Speaking 5, page 208*

LISTENING 2: Tapping the Energy of Tides

VOCABULARY (15 minutes)

1. Have pairs match words with definitions.
2. Check answers as a class, and then have pairs write model sentences for each vocabulary item.
3. Direct volunteers to read their sentences. Compare sentences for the same words and make corrections as necessary.

> **Vocabulary Answers, p. 208-209**
> **1.** b; **2.** c; **3.** a; **4.** b; **5.** b; **6.** c;
> **7.** a; **8.** a; **9.** b; **10.** c; **11.** b; **12.** b

MULTILEVEL OPTION

Place students in mixed-level pairs. Have higher-level students assist lower-level students in selecting the definition and explaining the meaning of the words. Direct students to alternate reading the sentences aloud and help each other with pronunciation.

 For additional practice with the vocabulary, have students visit *Q Online Practice*.

▶ *Listening and Speaking 5, page 209*

PREVIEW LISTENING 2 (5 minutes)

1. Direct students' attention to the photo and ask: *How do you think we can harness energy from the sea? Could this type of energy be used everywhere? Why or why not?*

2. Direct students to write advantages and disadvantages of using tidal energy.

3. Tell students they should review their answers after the Listening.

Listening 2 Background Note

Records of humans harnessing the power of the tides dates back to the 8th century, where evidence of devices meant to capture energy from the ocean were found off the coast of Western European countries. So it's hardly a new source of energy. However, it is an underutilized source of energy. There is enough energy flowing within the tides of the oceans to provide power for all of the world. The American Council on Renewable Energy figures that there is 450,000 megawatts of energy in the ocean, which is 1,000 times the energy available from wind—partly because water is much denser than air. Countries with extensive coastlines could benefit greatly from increased study of this energy source.

Teaching Note

Students may find the following words or phrases difficult.

in its infancy: (phr.) the early development of something

start-up: (n.) a company that is just beginning to operate, especially an Internet company

deflected: (adj.) turned away from

trivial: (adj.) not important or serious; not worth considering

▶ *Listening and Speaking 5, page 210*

LISTEN FOR MAIN IDEAS (15 minutes)

🔊 CD4, Track 6

1. Preview the questions with the class.

2. Pair students and have them predict what they think the answer to each question might be.

3. Play the audio and have students complete the activity individually.

4. Direct students to compare their answers with a partner, and ask students to compare the correct answers with their predicted answers.

5. Check answers as a class.

Listen for Main Idea Answers, p. 210

1. Tidal power is renewable; it's reliable and very powerful.

2. He means that global warming is a big problem and there is not just one solution, but using tidal power can help.

3. New Hampshire could get enough power for 36,000 homes or more.

4. The technology is experimental and expensive; the turbines might cause problems with the fishing industry.

LISTEN FOR DETAILS (10 minutes)

🔊 CD4, Track 7

1. Direct students to read the statements before they listen again.

2. As you play the audio, have students listen and circle the answer to complete each statement.

3. Have students compare answers with a partner.

4. Replay the audio so that partners can check their answers.

5. Go over the answers with the class.

Listen for Details Answers, pp. 210-211
1. renewable
2. 20
3. supporters
4. tidal
5. windmills
6. more
7. Two
8. safely pass through
9. disagree
10. cannot

 For additional practice with listening comprehension, have students visit *Q Online Practice*.

▶ *Listening and Speaking 5, page 211*

WHAT DO YOU THINK?

A (15 minutes)

1. Ask students to read the questions and reflect on their answers.

2. Seat students in small groups and assign roles: a group leader to make sure everyone contributes, a note-taker to record the group's ideas, a reporter to share the group's ideas with the class, and a timekeeper to watch the clock.

3. Give students five minutes to discuss the questions. Call time if conversations are winding down. Allow them an extra minute or two if necessary.

4. Call on each group's reporter to share ideas with the class.

Activity A Answers, p. 211
Possible answers:
1. I'm convinced that tidal power is reliable, but I'm not convinced that it can generate enough power.
2. Tidal energy can be a good source of energy for countries with a lot of coastline, like Japan.
3. Tidal power will be able to compete with oil, because oil is a limited resource but the tides will be with us forever.

B (10 minutes)

1. Have students continue working in their small groups to discuss the questions in Activity B. Tell them to choose a new leader, recorder, reporter, and timekeeper.

2. Call on the new reporter to share the group's answers to the questions.

Critical Q: Expansion Activity

Interpret (10 minutes)

CD4, Track 3
1. Read the Critical Thinking Tip from page 211.
2. Ask the class: *In what situations do you think it's important to interpret what other people might think? Why?* Then say: *We're going to practice interpreting what other people think by reviewing Listening 1.*
3. Pair students and write the following question on the board: *Would Emily Regan or Jay Chen support tidal energy? Why or why not?* Play Listening 1 and direct students to take notes that will support their answers.
4. Then have pairs discuss their interpretations and share with the class.

Learning Outcome

Use the learning outcome to frame the purpose and relevance of Listenings 1 and 2 and the Critical Q activity. Ask: *What did you learn from Listenings 1 and 2 and the Critical Q that prepares you to participate in a class debate on the future of energy?*

▶ *Listening and Speaking 5, page 212*

Vocabulary Skill: Greek and Latin word roots (10 minutes)

1. Present the information on the Vocabulary Skill. Call on volunteers to read the examples aloud.
2. Check comprehension: *What is a root? How can learning Greek and Latin roots be helpful?*

Skill Note

Greek and Latin roots are valuable for vocabulary acquisition because they help learners efficiently process new words. They are especially helpful to know when learning academic vocabulary and processing information from different subject areas. The following chart gives a sample of some roots that are likely to appear in different subject areas.

Subject area	Roots
Math	*graph* (write), *fract* (break), *meter* (measure), *var* (different), *loc* (place), *fer* (carry)
Science	*bio* (life), *cog* (to know), *circum* (around), *cont* (to join), *corp* (body), *derm* (skin), *duc* (to lead), *hyper* (over), *vital* (life)

A (10 minutes)

1. Preview the instructions and model the activity by reviewing the example as a class.
2. Direct students to complete the activity individually. Circulate around the room as needed.
3. Ask students to check their answers with a partner. Then discuss answers as a class.

Activity A Answers, pp. 212-213
1. a; **2.** b; **3.** a; **4.** a; **5.** b; **6.** a; **7.** a

▶ *Listening and Speaking 5, page 213*

B (10 minutes)

1. Preview the directions with the class.
2. Model the activity by completing the task for "auto" on the board as a class.
3. Pair students to complete the activity.
4. Have pairs compare their words.

Activity B Answers, p. 213
Answers will vary.

C (10 minutes)

1. Direct students to write their sentences and then read them to a partner. The partner should guess the word with the Greek or Latin root and its meaning.

2. Choose volunteers to write sentences on the board. Correct as needed.

Activity C Answers, p. 213
Answers will vary.

 For additional practice with words with Greek and Latin word roots, have students visit *Q Online Practice*.

▶ *Listening and Speaking 5, page 214*

SPEAKING

Grammar: Adverb clauses (15 minutes)

1. Present the information on the Grammar Skill. Probe for prior knowledge by asking: *When have you seen this grammar form used before? When do you use it in your own speech?*

2. Check comprehension. Ask: *What is an adverb clause? What can you tell me about adverb clauses that express reason? That show contrast? Which subordinators should you be careful of? Why?*

Skill Note

Point out some of the reasons why adverb clauses are used. For example, adverb clauses that express reasons are used in situations where people need to explain a decision, consider pros and cons of an argument, or argue for a particular point of view. Adverb clauses that show concession are used in situations where people need to explain why one choice is better than another or why an effort didn't quite succeed. Invite students to brainstorm more situations in which each type of clause is used.

▶ *Listening and Speaking 5, page 215*

A (10 minutes)

🔊 CD4, Track 8

1. Direct students to circle *reason* or *concession* for the relationship they hear in each statement.

2. Play the audio.

3. Put students in pairs to discuss their answers.

4. Call on volunteers to share their ideas.

Activity A Answers, p. 215
1. a. reason
2. a. reason
3. b. concession
4. b. concession
5. a. reason
6. b. concession

Tip for Success (5 minutes)

1. Read the tip aloud.

2. Ask students to practice this pronunciation tip with sentences from the skill box. Model for clarity.

B (5 minutes)

1. Have a volunteer read the directions to the activity.

2. As a class, choose the completion for the first statement.

3. Ask pairs to complete the remainder of the task and practice the conversations.

4. Check answers as a class.

Activity B Answers, p. 215
1. A: Even though; B: due to the fact that
2. A: Because; B: in spite of the fact that
3. A: as; B: although; because

▶ *Listening and Speaking 5, page 216*

C (15 minutes)

1. Place students into pairs, and have then preview the task. Elicit questions they may have.

2. Direct students to create and practice their conversations. Offer support as needed.

3. Have each pair present one conversation to the class.

 For additional practice with adverb clauses, have students visit *Q Online Practice*.

Pronunciation: Sentence rhythm
(10 minutes)

🔊 CD4, Track 9

1. Probe students' prior knowledge by asking: *What do you already know about sentence rhythm?*

2. Present the information on the Pronunciation Skill, playing the audio at the highlighted points.

3. Check comprehension. Ask: *What features combine to create sentence rhythm? What can you do to sound natural when speaking English?*

4. Have students practice reading the example rhythm patterns listed in the Pronunciation Skill box.

▶ *Listening and Speaking 5, page 217*

A (5–10 minutes)

🔊 CD4, Track 10

1. Preview the instructions for the task.

2. Play the audio and have students complete the task individually.

3. Check answers as a class.

4. Play the audio a second time, and have students speak along with the audio.

5. Pair students and direct them to take turns reading the text aloud, focusing on where to place stress.

B (15 minutes)

🔊 CD4, Track 11

1. Preview the directions, and model the activity by completing the first statement together.

2. Direct students to complete the task in pairs.

3. Play the audio and have students check their answers, making corrections as needed.

4. Ask students to practice the conversation.

> **Activity B Answers, p. 217**
> A: Did you see the <u>energy</u> <u>debate</u> on <u>TV</u> last <u>night</u>?
> B: <u>No</u>, I should have <u>watched</u> it, but I had to <u>study</u> for a <u>math</u> test. Give me the <u>highlights</u>.
> A: Well, it was the <u>big</u> <u>oil</u> <u>companies</u> versus the environmentalists.
> B: <u>Which</u> side had the best <u>arguments</u>?
> A: <u>Both</u> sides presented <u>good</u> <u>cases</u>. The <u>oil</u> companies had more <u>research</u>, but the <u>environmentalists</u> made <u>more</u> <u>compelling</u> <u>arguments</u>. They <u>convinced</u> me that some of the <u>oil</u> companies' <u>efforts</u> are really <u>misguided</u> and that our <u>reliance</u> on <u>fossil</u> fuels <u>has</u> to <u>end</u>.
> B: Was it possible to tell who <u>won</u> the <u>debate</u>?
> A: Not <u>really</u>. Because the issues are <u>so</u> <u>controversial</u>, I think it's <u>hard</u> to come to any <u>real</u> <u>resolution</u>. I <u>recorded</u> it, so I'm going to <u>watch</u> it <u>again</u>.
> B: There <u>aren't</u> any <u>easy</u> <u>answers</u>, <u>that's</u> for <u>sure</u>. Well, I'd like to <u>watch</u> that <u>recording</u> of the <u>debate</u> with you. It sounds <u>thought</u>-provoking.
> A: <u>Sure</u>. And I think it will be <u>useful</u> for our <u>class</u> <u>discussion</u> this <u>week</u>.

Tip for Success (2 minutes)

1. Choose a volunteer to read the tip aloud.

2. Ask students to identify where in the conversation in Activity A they see the tip in practice.

 For additional practice with sentence rhythm, have students visit *Q Online Practice*.

▶ *Listening and Speaking 5, page 218*

Speaking Skill: Debating opinions
(5 minutes)

1. Choose volunteers to read aloud the information on the Speaking Skill.

2. Check comprehension: *How can you keep a conversation going? What are some phrases to show agreement? To concede a point and then disagree? Why do you think a speaker would want to concede a point and then disagree?*

A (10 minutes)

🔊 CD4, Track 12

1. Preview the directions to the activity.

2. Direct students to complete the task individually.

3. Play the audio.

4. Have students compare answers with a partner. Then check answers as a class.

> **Activity A Answers, pp. 218-219**
> 1. Although I agree
> 2. many scientists disagree
> 3. That's true
> 4. You raise an important point
> 5. the fact of the matter is
> 6. While I also found
> 7. most experts argue
> 8. Environmentalists believe
> 9. I'd certainly agree
> 10. However, many would argue

▶ *Listening and Speaking 5, page 219*

B (10 minutes)

1. Pair students and direct them to complete the conversation.

2. Ask pairs to practice their conversations. Invite volunteers to read aloud for the class.

Activity B Answers, pp. 219-220
Answers will vary. They should express the following:
1. You might be right, but (disagreement)
2. While that is true, it's clear that (disagreement)
3. I couldn't agree more (agreement)
4. You might be right, but (disagreement)
5. While that is true, it's clear that (disagreement)
6. I see what you're saying, but (disagreement)

▶ *Listening and Speaking 5, page 220*

C (10 minutes)

Direct students to complete the task. Remind "Student B" to use pronunciation and speaking skills from the unit to react and express opinions.

 For additional practice with sentence rhythm, have students visit *Q Online Practice*.

Unit Assignment:
Debate the Future of Energy

Unit Question (5 minutes)

Refer students back to the ideas they discussed at the beginning of the unit about where the world's energy should come from. Cue students if necessary by asking specific questions about the content of the unit: *What energy sources did we learn about in this unit?*

Learning Outcome

1. Tie the Unit Assignment to the unit learning outcome. Say: *The outcome for this unit is to participate in a class debate in which you support opinions concerning the future of energy. This Unit Assignment is going to let you show your skill by engaging in a debate.*

2. Explain that you are going to use a rubric similar to their self-assessment rubric on p. 222 to grade their Unit Assignment. You can also share a copy of the Unit Assignment Rubric (on p. 97 of this *Teacher's Handbook*) with students.

▶ *Listening and Speaking 5, page 221*
Consider the Ideas (10 minutes)

A (10 minutes)

Direct students to complete the task individually.

B (10 minutes)

1. Place students into groups of four, and direct them to discuss the questions.

2. When the conversations have tapered off, ask a volunteer to lead a class discussion of the questions.

▶ *Listening and Speaking 5, page 222*
Prepare and Speak

Gather Ideas

A (20 minutes)

1. Have students work in their same groups of four to complete the activity.

2. Preview the directions and the steps to complete the activity. Elicit and answer questions students have.

3. Direct groups to begin the activity. Circulate around the room to provide support and examples.

4. Once they've written their arguments and defenses, have teams compare their answers with another team that has the same argument.

Organize Ideas

B (20 minutes)

1. Direct students to read through the debate format.

2. Ask students to close their books and give an impromptu quiz. Ask: *What do the people who go first say? How long do they talk? What's the next step? How long does it last? What's the final step? How long does it last?*

Speak

C (20 minutes)

1. Have groups conduct their debates.

2. Use the Unit Assignment Rubric on p. 97 of this *Teacher's Handbook* to score each student's presentation.

3. Alternatively, divide the class into large groups and have students give their presentations to their group. Have listeners complete the Unit Assignment Rubric.

Alternative Unit Assignments

Assign or have students choose one of these assignments to do instead of, or in addition to, the Unit Assignment.

1. Compare the attitude your friends, family, and neighbors had about energy consumption in the past with their views and actions today.

2. Discuss your view of the best way we can provide the energy for industrial and personal use while still protecting the environment.

3. Explain the steps your government has taken to regulate energy resources and environmental impacts.

 For an additional unit assignment, have students visit *Q Online Practice*.

Check and Reflect

Check

A (10 minutes)

1. Direct students to read and complete the self-assessment rubric.

2. Ask for a show of hands for how many students gave all or mostly *yes* answers.

3. Congratulate them on their success. Remind students that they can refer to the rubric before they begin the Unit Assignment so they can focus on the skills needed to do well. Have them discuss with a partner what they can improve.

▶ *Listening and Speaking 5, page 223*

Reflect

B (5-10 minutes)

Ask students to consider the questions in pairs or groups of three. When the conversations have tapered off, ask: *What aspects of the class debate helped you understand the material from the unit better? How?*

Track Your Success (5 minutes)

1. Have students circle the words they have learned in this unit. Suggest that students go back through the unit to review any words they have forgotten.

2. Have students check the skills they have mastered. If students need more practice to feel confident about their proficiency in a skill, point out the page numbers and encourage them to review.

3. Read the Learning Outcome aloud. Ask students if they feel that they have met the outcome.

Unit Assignment Rubric

Student name: _____

Date: _____

20 points = Presentation element was completely successful (at least 90% of the time).
15 points = Presentation element was mostly successful (at least 70% of the time).
10 points = Presentation element was partially successful (at least 50% of the time).
 0 points = Presentation element was not successful.

Debate the Future of Energy	20 points	15 points	10 points	0 points
Student spoke clearly and at a good speed about the topic.				
Student used adverbial clauses appropriately.				
Student used five vocabulary words from the unit.				
Student used appropriate stress on words and syllables in their speech.				
Student agreed and disagreed with opinions appropriately.				

Total points: _____

Comments:

UNIT 10

Unit QUESTION
Is bigger always better?

Size and Scale

LISTENING • listening for pros and cons
VOCABULARY • connotations
GRAMMAR • parallel structure
PRONUNCIATION • word stress patterns
SPEAKING • developing interview skills

LEARNING OUTCOME

Role-play interviews for a job or a school and be prepared to answer a question that is creative or unusual.

▶ *Listening and Speaking 5, page 225*

Preview the Unit

Learning Outcome

1. Ask for a volunteer to read the unit skills, then the unit learning outcome.

2. Explain: *This is what you are expected to be able to do by the unit's end. The learning outcome explains how you are going to be evaluated. With this outcome in mind, you should focus on learning these skills (Listening, Vocabulary, Grammar, Pronunciation, Speaking) that will support your goal of "role-playing interviews for a job or a school." This can also help you act as mentors in the classroom to help the other students meet this outcome.*

A (10 minutes)

1. Ask the class: *Do you like restaurants to serve big or small portions? Are you attracted to big or small cars?*

2. Put students in pairs or small groups to discuss the first two questions.

3. Call on volunteers to share their ideas with the class. Ask questions: *Have you been a part of a small or large business? Which do you prefer? Why? Do you prefer to have a large group of friends or a smaller group?*

4. Focus students' attention on the photo. Have a volunteer describe the photo to the class. Read the question aloud. Ask: *What are advantages and disadvantages to buying household items in large quantities?*

Activity A Answers, p. 225
Possible answers:
1. A small business can give its employees the sense of being an important part of something. A large business, however, can offer better benefits and resources.
2. I prefer to be in a small group because it's easier to talk with everyone and have meaningful conversations.
3. I prefer small stores because I usually know everyone in the store and enjoy talking with them while I shop. I like bigger stores because they usually have everything that I'm looking for.

B (10 minutes)

1. Read the Unit Question aloud. Give students a minute to silently consider their answers to the question. Then ask students who would answer *yes* to stand on one side of the room and students who would answer *no* to stand on the other side of the room.

2. Direct students to tell a partner next to them their reasons for choosing that side of the issue.

3. Call on volunteers from each side to share their opinions with the class.

4. After students have shared their opinions, provide an opportunity for anyone who would like to change sides to do so.

5. Ask students to sit down, copy the Unit Question, and make a note of their answers and reasons. They will refer to these notes at the end of the unit.

Activity B Answers, p. 225
Possible answers:
Bigger is better because you can get a better value if you are buying something. Less is better because then you appreciate it more.

The Q Classroom (5 minutes)

CD4, Track 13

1. Play The Q Classroom. Use the example from the audio to help students continue the conversation. Ask: *How did the students answer the question? Do you agree or disagree with their ideas? Why?*

2. Say: *In the audio, Marcus says that there are more exciting opportunities in a big city. Do you agree with him? Why or why not?*

▶ *Listening and Speaking 5, page 226*

C (10 minutes)

1. Preview the instructions to the activity and ask students to look over the survey. Elicit questions.

2. Ask students to fill out the survey individually and tally their answers.

D (10 minutes)

1. Place students into groups and have them discuss their answers.

2. As a class, discuss reasons why students choose small colleges or large universities.

> **MULTILEVEL OPTION**
>
> Pair lower- and higher-level students. Have the higher-level students interview the lower-level students using the survey. Ask higher-level students to share the results with the class and lower-level students to tell if they agree with the results.

EXPANSION ACTIVITY: Making a Survey (15 minutes)

1. Place students into pairs and direct them to create a survey based upon the Unit Question. Have them brainstorm questions for determining if they think bigger is always better (e.g., *What do you do if you get too much food at a restaurant? When is more worse than less?*)

2. Place pairs into larger groups and have them survey each other and record their answers. Discuss some of the student's answers as a class.

LISTENING

▶ *Listening and Speaking 5, page 227*

LISTENING 1: Small Is the New Big

VOCABULARY (10 minutes)

1. Repeat each bolded vocabulary item three times, modeling pronunciation, and ask students to repeat.

2. Complete the activity as a class, choosing a volunteer to read each statement, and select the best way to complete the sentence.

3. Ask the class to decide if the sentences have been completed correctly. Correct as needed.

> **MULTILEVEL OPTION**
>
> Pair lower- and higher-level students to complete the statements. Check answers as a class. Challenge higher-level students to define the words and lower-level students to give their part of speech.

Vocabulary Answers, p. 227-228
1. close contact between
2. easy online applications
3. given at the same time
4. guiding belief
5. investigate
6. fired
7. if the product will succeed
8. have equal qualities or characteristics
9. adapt to
10. other organizations or countries
11. can't
12. put money into

 For additional practice with the vocabulary, have students visit *Q Online Practice*.

▶ *Listening and Speaking 5, page 228*

PREVIEW LISTENING 1 (5 minutes)

1. Direct students to look at the photos. Ask: *What are advantages of big computers? Of small computers? Why?*

2. Direct students to read and predict what the speaker will say. Tell students they should review their guesses after the Listening.

Listening 1 Background Note

"Economies of scale" is a term that refers to the idea that as a company expands, the cost of operating that business goes down. For example, a business that ships 100 packages a month pays a higher price per package to ship than one who ships 100,000 packages a month, because the larger company can leverage the volume it ships to obtain lower shipping costs. Amazon, an online store, is an example of an economy of scale. The company, which was initially known as a bookseller but now sells computers, groceries, and clothing, ships most items for free if a customer buys $25 worth of merchandise. A small business cannot offer free shipping because the scale of its business isn't large enough. However, as Listening 1 will show, small companies have other unique advantages.

Teaching Note

Students may find the following words or phrases difficult.

marine: (n.) a soldier who is trained to serve on land or at sea, especially one in the US Marine Corps (an ex-marine is a former marine)

CEO: (n.) a Chief Executive Officer; the head of a company

The Fortune 500: (proper n.) a list published by Fortune magazine every year; it ranks the top 50 U.S. corporations, based on their overall income

R&D: (proper n.) the Research and Development department in a company

Enron: (proper n.) formerly one of the largest American energy companies; it went bankrupt in 2000 and its leaders were found guilty of accounting fraud. The company has become a symbol of corporate corruption.

Andersen: (proper n.) Arthur Andersen, formerly one of the "big five" American accounting firms; they went out of business in 2000 after facing criminal charges related to their role in the Enron audit.

cream: (v.) to completely defeat

boom box: (n.) a personal stereo system, usually one with speakers and a handle for carrying it

Craigslist: (proper n.) a website where people can buy and sell goods and services

eBay: (proper n.) an online auction site; a website where people can buy and sell goods

LISTEN FOR MAIN IDEAS (10 minutes)

 CD4, Track 14

1. Preview the instructions and the statements together as a class.

2. Play the audio and have students complete the activity individually.

3. Place students into pairs and have them check their answers.

> **Listen for Main Ideas Answers, pp. 228-229**
> Check items 1, 3, and 4.

▶ *Listening and Speaking 5, page 229*

LISTEN FOR DETAILS (10 minutes)

 CD4, Track 15

1. Direct students to preview the questions before listening to the audio.

2. As you play the audio, have students listen and answer the questions.

3. Have students compare answers with a partner.

4. Discuss answers with the class.

> **Listen for Details Answers, pp. 229-230**
> 1. Made a fortune; had power, profit, and growth; controlled supply and markets; were faster and more efficient; were more trusted
> 2. Because they use a lot of power and are not as efficient as networked computers
> 3. Big-screen TVs
> 4. How a small company wanted to do something and could do it without a lot of meetings, time, or money
> 5. It seems to mean that big companies end up lying to their customers on their websites.
> 6. They might outsource manufacturing and billing jobs so they can focus on the big ideas.
> 7. Godin means that small companies can invest in what they want to because they don't have to listen to corporate leaders or bosses.
> 8. Godin would say it is better to be the head of Craigslist, a smaller company.

 For additional practice with listening comprehension, have students visit *Q Online Practice*.

WHAT DO YOU THINK? (10 minutes)

1. Ask students to read the questions and reflect on their answers.

2. Seat students in small groups and assign roles: a group leader to make sure everyone contributes, a note-taker to record the group's ideas, a reporter to share the group's ideas with the class, and a timekeeper to watch the clock.

3. Give students five minutes to discuss the questions. Call time if conversations are winding down. Allow them an extra minute or two if necessary.

4. Call on each group's reporter to share ideas with the class.

> **What Do You Think? Answers, p. 230**
> Possible answers:
> **1.** The expression means that small things, like companies, are able to innovate more than large companies.
> **2.** I agree because smaller companies are able to make new paths in the marketplace that big companies, being established brands, cannot.
> **3.** I'd rather work for a smaller company because I'd be able to see the result of my work a lot more clearly than if I worked for a big company.

Learning Outcome

Use the learning outcome to frame the purpose and relevance of Listening 1. Ask: *What did you learn from Listening 1 that prepares you to role-play interviews for a job?*

▶ *Listening and Speaking 5, page 231*

Listening Skill: Listening for pros and cons (10 minutes)

 CD4, Track 16

1. Present the information in the Listening Skill box. Play the highlighted audio at the appropriate time.

2. Check comprehension by asking questions: *How does a speaker signal he or she will discuss pros and cons? How can a T-chart help you when listening to a lecture that includes pros and cons? What organizational cues signal pros and cons?*

▶ *Listening and Speaking 5, page 232*

A (10 minutes)
CD4, Track 17

1. Ask a volunteer to read the instructions aloud.

2. Play the audio and direct students to fill in the T-chart as they listen.

3. Pair students to compare answers, then check answers as a class.

> **Listening Skill A Answers, p. 232**

Small Town		Big City	
Pros	**Cons**	**Pros**	**Cons**
*familiar *owned a car *open space to play *convenient knowing everyone	*lack of jobs *no public transport-ation *not exciting	*more jobs *public transport-ation so no need for car *exciting	*unknown *more expensive *difficulties of public transpor-tation *busy streets

B (10 minutes)
CD4, Track 17

1. Play the audio and direct students to write the organizational cues as they listen.

2. Check answers as a class.

> **Listening Skill B Answers, p. 232**
> in contrast to; however; on the one hand; on the other hand

 For additional practice with listening to pros and cons, have students visit *Q Online Practice*.

LISTENING 2: Sizing Up Colleges: One Size Does Not Fit All

VOCABULARY (20 minutes)

1. Read the directions. Complete the first item as a class.

2. Put students into groups of three and assign roles: one reader, one decider, and one writer. The reader reads the sentence, the decider chooses which definition is correct for the bolded word, and the writer writes the answer.

3. After the groups have chosen their answers, allow a little time to debate the answers the decider chose.

4. Check answers as a class.

> **Vocabulary Answers, pp. 232-233**
> **1.** b; **2.** a; **3.** a; **4.** c; **5.** a; **6.** b;
> **7.** b; **8.** c; **9.** a; **10.** c; **11.** c; **12.** b

For additional practice with the vocabulary, have students visit *Q Online Practice*.

PREVIEW LISTENING 2 (5 minutes)

1. Direct students' attention to the photos and ask: *What does it mean when we talk about large and small universities? What can one offer students that the other cannot?*

2. Preview the instructions and the phrases for the Venn diagram.

3. Place students into pairs and direct them to fill in the Venn diagram.

4. Place pairs into larger groups to discuss the similarities and differences in their choices.

5. Tell students they should review their Venn diagrams after the Listening.

Listening 2 Background Note

University of Michigan offers a wide array of majors, such as public policy, anthropology, chemistry, dance, Islamic studies, law, and pharmacology—among many others. The school boasts many successful college sports teams and an enrollment of 41,000 undergraduate and graduate students.

Oberlin College, on the other hand, offers fewer degrees but has well-known programs in music, Russian, theatre, dance, and Jewish studies. Oberlin boasts the oldest music conservatory in the United States and eight degree programs within the conservatory. The yearly enrollment at the conservatory of Oberlin is 615 students—and there are only 3,000 students in the entire college.

Teaching Note

Students may find the following words or phrases difficult.

rah rah: (adj.) very enthusiastic about something

red tape: (phr.) official rules that seem more complicated than necessary and prevent things from being done quickly

alumnus: (n.) a former male student of a school, college, or university (female: alumna; plural: alumni)

LISTEN FOR MAIN IDEAS (10 minutes)

CD4, Track 18

1. Preview the instructions and each of the questions.

2. Play the audio and have students complete the activity individually.

3. Pair students to have them compare answers. Then discuss answers as a class.

Listen for Main Idea Answers, p. 235
1. To give advice to students preparing to choose a college and to point out pros and cons of each
2. The size of the college and the student's personality and academic goals
3. Areas of facilities and research, extracurricular activities, contact with professors, and class size
4. The subtitle suggests that not everyone will want to attend a college of the same size.

LISTEN FOR DETAILS (10 minutes)

CD4, Track 19

A (10 minutes)

1. Direct students to preview the T-chart before they listen again.

2. As you play the audio, have students listen and place the details into the T-chart.

3. Have students compare answers with a partner.

Listen for Details A Answers, p. 235
Pros: endless options and countless <u>degree</u> programs; access to <u>research</u> facilities; <u>distinguished</u> professors
Cons: courses taught by <u>teaching assistants (TAs)</u>, not professors; professors focused on <u>research/ publishing/ graduate students</u> rather than teaching; introductory classes with <u>hundreds</u> of students

B (10 minutes)
CD4, Track 19

1. Direct students to preview the T-chart on small schools before they listen again.

2. As you play the audio, have students listen and place the details into the T-chart.

3. Have students compare answers with a partner.

Listen for Details B Answers, p. 236
Pros: hands-on learning opportunities; <u>small</u> class sizes; classes taught by <u>professors</u>; high level of <u>student-teacher</u> interaction
Cons: <u>fewer</u> research facilities; no <u>graduate</u> students to interact with; limited sporting events and other <u>extracurricular</u> activities

 For additional practice with listening comprehension, have students visit *Q Online Practice*.

Q WHAT DO YOU THINK?

A (10 minutes)

1. Ask students to read the questions and reflect on their answers.

2. Seat students in small groups and assign roles: a group leader to make sure everyone contributes, a note-taker to record the group's ideas, a reporter to share the group's ideas with the class, and a timekeeper to watch the clock.

3. Give students five minutes to discuss the questions. Call time if conversations are winding down. Allow them an extra minute or two if necessary.

4. Call on each group's reporter to share ideas with the class.

Activity A Answers, p. 236
Possible answers:
1. The most important advice the College Board gives is to see who is actually teaching the classes.
2. The school that I am at is close to my home, and that was the biggest factor since I wanted to stay close to my family. I think it was the right choice for me.

Critical Q: Expansion Activity

Incorporate (15 minutes)

1. Read the Critical Thinking Tip from page 236.
2. Ask students: *Is bigger always better? Why or why not?* Say: *Look at the activities you completed for Listenings 1 and 2 and use what the speakers said about big and small institutions in a statement to explain your answer.*
3. Ask students to review their work based on the Listenings. Then have students work with a partner that shares their opinion.
4. Direct the pairs to craft one statement, up to three minutes in length, that incorporates the information from the Listenings to support their opinion.
5. Place pairs into larger groups and have each pair read their statement to the group. Choose a few volunteers to share their statements with the class.

B (5 minutes)

1. Have students continue working in their small groups to discuss the questions in Activity B. Tell them to choose a new leader, recorder, reporter, and timekeeper.

2. Call on the new reporter to share the group's answers to the questions.

Learning Outcome

Use the learning outcome to frame the purpose and relevance of Listenings 1 and 2 and the Critical Q activity. Ask: *What did you learn from Listenings 1 and 2 and the Critical Q that prepares you to role-play interviews for a job or a school?*

▶ *Listening and Speaking 5, page 237*

Vocabulary Skill: Connotations (10 minutes)

1. Present the information on connotations by choosing a volunteer to read the text aloud.

2. Check comprehension: *What is a denotation? What is a connotation? What's an example of a connotation?*

Skill Note

Connotations can introduce meanings into speech that the learner of English never meant. In fact, a thesaurus can sometimes lead learners to say or write things that others might find offensive. For example, when looking up the word *quiet* in a thesaurus, the synonym *mute* connotes that a person is not willing to talk—as opposed to not talking very much. Emphasize the difference between the sentences "She remained quiet throughout the evening," and "She remained mute throughout the evening." Point out that in addition to connotation, speakers use tone of voice to note whether the word they are saying is positive or negative. Negative words are sometimes emphasized or drawn out, as in "She certainly seems *quiet*."

A (10 minutes)

1. Direct students to complete the activity with a partner. Have students use a dictionary to check their work.

2. Go over the answers with the class. Provide example sentences to illustrate the negative or positive connotations.

Unit 10   **103**

Activity A Answers, p. 237

1. +passion	-obsession
2. + economical	-cheap
3. -fire	+downsize
4. +assertive	-pushy
5. +smile	-smirk
6. -nerdy	+studious
7. -notorious	+distinguished
8. -gossip	+talk
9. -lazy	+relaxed
10. +persistence	-stubbornness

▶ *Listening and Speaking 5, page 238*

B (10 minutes)

1. Preview the instructions and place students into pairs.

2. Model the activity by completing the first statement as a class.

3. Direct students to complete the task.

4. Check answers and discuss ideas as a class.

Activity B Answers, p. 238

1. cheap;   **2.** persistence;   **3.** gossip;

4. relaxed;   **5.** notorious;   **6.** smirk

7. downsize;   **8.** assertive

MULTILEVEL OPTION

Pair lower-level students with higher-level students. Direct the higher-level students to create additional sentences (using additional words from Activity A) for the lower-level students to fill in based on connotation.

 For additional practice with connotations, have students visit *Q Online Practice*.

▶ *Listening and Speaking 5, page 239*

SPEAKING

Grammar: Parallel structure (20 minutes)

◉) CD4, Track 20

1. Present the information on parallel structure to students, playing the audio at the highlighted point.

2. Check comprehension by asking questions: *What is parallel structure? When do we use it? How can you help yourself hear when a parallel structure has been broken? How do people use tone of voice when listing single items? Phrases?*

3. Point out that it is important to know the different types of sentences because, as students will see in the next section, each type has its own intonation.

Tip for Success (3 minutes)

1. Read the tip aloud.

2. Ask students to share a few example sentences that reduce clauses to phrases.

Skill Note

Why do phrases in a list have to be parallel? Symmetry of language helps listeners follow ideas. When that symmetry isn't expressed in parallel structures, it can be confusing. Often listeners have to stop listening to the speaker and focus on reinterpreting what was said. At that point, communication can break down, and the speaker will have to repeat herself.

▶ *Listening and Speaking 5, page 240*

A (10 minutes)

◉) CD4, Track 21

1. Direct students to listen to the audio and complete the task individually.

2. Play the audio.

3. Call on volunteers to share their ideas with the class. Correct and replay the audio, as needed.

Activity A Answers, p. 240

1. parallel	**2.** not parallel
3. parallel	**4.** not parallel
5. parallel	**6.** parallel
7. parallel	**8.** not parallel
9. parallel	**10.** not parallel

B (10 minutes)

1. Place students into pairs and have them complete the activity. Remind students they must use lists in their speech.

2. Circulate around the room to offer support and corrections as needed.

Activity B Answers, p. 240
Answers will vary.

 For additional practice with parallel structures, have students visit *Q Online Practice*.

▶ Listening and Speaking 5, page 241

Pronunciation: Word stress patterns
(15 minutes)

 CD4, Track 22

1. Present the information to students, playing the audio at the highlighted point.

2. Check comprehension by asking questions: *What is a common word stress pattern for nouns? What does the number 2-1 signify? 3-2?*

3. Practice word stress patterns by pairing students and asking them to practice reading the examples.

▶ Listening and Speaking 5, page 242

A (10 minutes)
CD4, Track 23

1. Preview the instructions and the words. Model how to use the numbering system by completing the first item together (conducted 3-2).

2. Direct students to complete the activity individually.

3. Play the audio.

4. Direct the class to check answers and practice pronunciation with a partner when done.

5. Choose volunteers to write the answers on the board and explain their choices. Correct as needed.

> **Activity A Answers, p. 242**
> **1.** 3-2 **2.** 2-1 **3.** 4-3 **4.** 4-2 **5.** 3-2 **6.** 2-2
> **7.** 4-3 **8.** 3-1 **9.** 3-2 **10.** 2-1 **11.** 3-1 **12.** 3-1

Tip for Success (2 minutes)

1. Read the tip aloud.

2. Ask: *How could organizing words by their stress patterns and practicing them help you?*

B (10 minutes)

1. Direct students to alternate saying the words aloud with a partner and fill in the chart.

2. Check answers as a class. Model pronunciation and elicit corrections as necessary.

> **Activity B Answers, p. 242**
> 2-1: clever, gifted, honest
> 2-2: mature, unique
> 3-1: confident, organized, passionate, sociable, talented
> 3-2: creative, efficient
> 3-3: x
> 4-1: motivated
> 4-2: dependable, experienced, intelligent, reliable
> 4-3: conscientious, energetic, independent

▶ Listening and Speaking 5, page 243

C (10 minutes)

1. Place students into partners for the role-play.

2. Model the role-play by reading through the example for the class.

3. Direct students to begin. Circulate around the room to monitor progress.

web⁺ For additional practice with word stress patterns, have students visit *Q Online Practice*.

Speaking Skill: Developing interview skills (10 minutes)

1. Present the information on developing interview skills to the class.

2. Check comprehension: *What are the 3 P's you should complete before the interview? What should you do during the interview?* Tell students that for their Unit Assignment they will role-play an interview, so they will be using these skills.

▶ Listening and Speaking 5, page 244

A (10 minutes)
 CD4, Track 24

1. Place students into groups of four and preview the instructions.

2. Play the audio and have students take notes.

3. Direct the groups to discuss the questions.

> **Activity A Answers, p. 244**
> Answers will vary but may include:
> Candidate 2 is the best choice—sounds professional, uses parallel structure, and sounds enthusiastic.
> Candidate 1 doesn't seem to understand the question, and gives a vague answer.
> Candidate 3 uses informal speech and slang.

B (15 minutes)

1. Preview the instructions, place students into pairs, and direct them to complete the task. Circulate around the room and offer support as needed.

2. Choose a few pairs to present their interview situation to the class.

web⁺ For additional practice with developing interview skills, have students visit *Q Online Practice*.

Q° **Unit Assignment:** Role-Play interviews for a job or a school

Unit Question (5 minutes)

Refer students back to the ideas they discussed at the beginning of the unit about the value of bigger. Cue students if necessary by asking specific questions about the content of the unit: *Do small businesses have advantages over big businesses? What about small schools over big schools? Is small the new big, or is bigger always better?*

Learning Outcome

1. Tie the Unit Assignment to the unit learning outcome. Say: *The outcome for this unit is to role-play interviews for a job or a school and be prepared to answer a question that is creative or unusual. This Unit Assignment is going to let you show your skill in conducting a role-play and answering questions.*

2. Explain that you are going to use a rubric similar to their self-assessment rubric on p. 246 to grade their Unit Assignment. You can also share a copy of the Unit Assignment Rubric (on p. 108 of this *Teacher's Handbook*) with students.

Consider the Ideas

A (5 minutes)

1. Place students into groups of six or more.
2. Direct the members of the groups to consider the questions and brainstorm answers silently.

▶ *Listening and Speaking 5, page 245*

B (10 minutes)

1. Direct the groups to consider the questions and discuss their ideas.
2. As a class, review some of the groups' answers.

Prepare and Speak

Gather Ideas

A (5–10 minutes)

1. Keep students in their same groups.
2. Preview the activity and direct groups to follow the steps to gather their ideas.

Organize Ideas

B (10 minutes)

1. Preview the instructions. Direct group members to decide which students will be interview committee members and which will be candidates.

2. Direct each smaller group to complete their task. Note to committee members that they will be dividing the questions amongst themselves to ask the candidates.

▶ *Listening and Speaking 5, page 246*

Speak

C (20 minutes)

1. Call on groups to role-play their interviews for the class.

2. Use the Unit Assignment Rubric on p. 108 of this *Teacher's Handbook* to score each student's role-play performance.

3. Alternatively, divide the class into two groups and have students perform their role-play for their group. Have listeners complete the Unit Assignment Rubric.

Alternative Unit Assignments

Assign or have students choose one of these assignments to do instead of, or in addition to, the Unit Assignment.

1. Choose your ideal job or school and explain why you chose it and why you are the best candidate.

2. Describe a small business in your area and compare it to a large business in your area and explain why both offer unique opportunities to their employees.

3. Compare your priorities for a place to work or study with those your parents think you should have.

 For an additional unit assignment, have students visit *Q Online Practice.*

Working efficiently together toward a common goal and sharing a common responsibility is a feature of successful teams. In the Unit Assignment, students had to work together to create a role-play as either an interview committee member or a job candidate, but the overarching goal—practicing interview skills—benefited all of the group members. Tell students that when all group members are aware of and committed to reaching the common goal, each step of the process becomes meaningful. Emphasize that visualizing the end objective as a group can help each individual work better together to get there.

Check and Reflect

Check

A (10 minutes)

1. Direct students to read and complete the self-assessment rubric.

2. Ask for a show of hands for how many students gave all or mostly yes answers.

3. Congratulate them on their success. Remind students that they can refer to the rubric before they begin the Unit Assignment so they can focus on the skills needed to do well. Have them discuss with a partner what they can improve.

▶ *Listening and Speaking 5, page 247*

Reflect

B (5–10 minutes)

Ask students to consider the questions in pairs or groups of three. When the conversations have tapered off, ask: *How did you feel asking or answering such creative and unusual questions? Did you have a technique for answering these questions? What was it? How did it help you?*

Track Your Success (5 minutes)

1. Have students circle the words they have learned in this unit. Suggest that students go back through the unit to review any words they have forgotten.

2. Have students check the skills they have mastered. If students need more practice to feel confident about their proficiency in a skill, point out the page numbers and encourage them to review.

3. Read the Learning Outcome aloud. Ask students if they feel that they have met the outcome.

Unit Assignment Rubric

Student name: _____

Date: _____

20 points = Presentation element was completely successful (at least 90% of the time).
15 points = Presentation element was mostly successful (at least 70% of the time).
10 points = Presentation element was partially successful (at least 50% of the time).
 0 points = Presentation element was not successful.

Role-Play Interviews for a Job or a School	20 points	15 points	10 points	0 points
Student spoke clearly and at a good speed about the topic.				
Student used vocabulary with appropriate connotations.				
Student used parallel structures when listing three or more items.				
Student stressed 2-, 3-, and 4- syllable words correctly.				
Student appeared relaxed and natural when interviewing and answering each other.				

Total points: _____

Comments:

Welcome to the Q Testing Program

1. MINIMUM SYSTEM REQUIREMENTS[1]

1024 x 768 screen resolution displaying 32-bit color

Web browser[2]:
Windows®-requires Internet Explorer® 7 or above
Mac®-requires OS X v10.4 and Safari® 2.0 or above
Linux®-requires Mozilla® 1.7 or Firefox® 1.5.0.9 or above

To open and use the customizable tests you must have an application installed that will open and edit .doc files, such as Microsoft® Word® (97 or higher).

To view and print the Print-and-go Tests, you must have an application installed that will open and print .pdf files, such as Adobe® Acrobat® Reader (6.0 or higher).

2. RUNNING THE APPLICATION

Windows®/Mac®
- Ensure that no other applications are running.
- Insert the Q: Skills for Success Testing Program CD-ROM into your CD-ROM drive.
- Double click on the file "start.htm" to start.

Linux®
- Insert the Q: Skills for Success Testing Program CD-ROM into your CD-ROM drive.
- Mount the disk on to the desktop.
- Double click on the CD-ROM icon.
- Right click on the icon for the "start.htm" file and select to "open with Mozilla".

3. TECHNICAL SUPPORT

If you experience any problems with this CD-ROM, please check that your machine matches or exceeds the minimum system requirements in point 1 above and that you are following the steps outlined in point 2 above.

If this does not help, e-mail us with your query at: elt.cdsupport.uk@oup.com
Be sure to provide the following information:

- Operating system (e.g. Windows 2000, Service Pack 4)
- Application used to access content, and version number
- Amount of RAM
- Processor speed
- Description of error or problem
- Actions before error occurred
- Number of times the error has occurred
- Is the error repeatable?

---

[1] The Q Testing Program CD-ROM also plays its audio files in a conventional CD player.

[2] Note that when browsing the CD-ROM in your Web browser, you must have pop-up windows enabled in your Web browser settings.

The Q Testing Program

The disc on the inside back cover of this book contains both ready-made and customizable versions of **Reading and Writing** and **Listening and Speaking** tests. Each of the tests consists of multiple choice, fill-in-the-blanks/sentence completion, error correction, sentence reordering/sentence construction, and matching exercises.

Creating and Using Tests

1. Select "Reading and Writing Tests" or "Listening and Speaking Tests" from the main menu.

2. Select the appropriate unit test or cumulative test (placement, midterm, or final) from the left-hand column.

3. For ready-made tests, select a Print-and-go Test, Answer Key, and Audio Script (for Listening and Speaking tests).

4. To modify tests for your students, select a Customizable Test, Answer Key, and Audio Script (for Listening and Speaking tests). Save the file to your computer and edit the test using Microsoft Word or a compatible word processor.

5. For Listening and Speaking tests, use the audio tracks provided with the tests. **Audio files for the listening and speaking tests can also be played in a standard CD player.**

Reading and Writing Tests

Each test consists of 40 questions taken from the selected unit. The Reading and Writing Tests assess reading skills, vocabulary, vocabulary skills, grammar, and writing skills.

Listening and Speaking Tests

Each test consists of 40 questions taken from the selected unit. The Listening and Speaking Tests assess listening skills, vocabulary, vocabulary skills, grammar, pronunciation, and speaking skills.

Cumulative Tests

The placement tests for both Listening and Speaking and Reading and Writing consist of 50 questions. Each placement test places students in the correct level of Q: Introductory–5. **A printable User Guide to help you administer the placement test is included with the placement test files on the CD-ROM.**

The midterm tests for both Listening and Speaking and Reading and Writing consist of 25 questions covering Units 1–5 of the selected Level. The midterm Reading and Listening texts are new and not used in any other tests or student books.

The final tests for both Listening and Speaking and Reading and Writing consist of 25 questions covering Units 6–10 of the selected Level. The final Reading and Listening texts are new and not used in any other tests or student books.